THE
INCREDIBLY
UNEXPECTED

*From High School Dropout
to College Graduate*

ANTHONY PERSEVERES

ISBN: 978-1-4834-7435-9 (sc)
ISBN: 978-1-4834-7434-2 (e)

Library of Congress Control Number: 2017913228

Lulu Publishing Services rev. date: 11/27/2017

To my sons,

Elijah and Isaiah.

Against all odds, bad cycles must be broken!

CONTENTS

ACKNOWLEDGMENTS

Anything I have ever done and will do well in my life I attribute to the support of my family and friends. No one has done anything great without some level of assistance from others. I am a better person because of the abundance of love given to me by a whole host of people. Thank you, Ronell, not just for being my lovely wife but also because during the countless hours, days, weeks, months, and years I toiled over this book, you always lent me your ear or a word of advice. Thanks for helping me come up with a cool book title. This book would've never seen the light of day without you. I love you to pieces. Thank you, mom, for showing me how to stick up for myself, advocate for what I deserve, and fight for what's right. Because of you, I am a force to be reckoned with.

Brother Jay, I may not totally understand the extent of what you're currently dealing with, but you're always in my thoughts. I hope to see you soon! Thank you, Janelle, Jolique, and Anjolique, for being my source of motivation. It is because of you three that I exist.

You guys mean the world to me. Thank you, Edwidge and Julande, for being among my best supporters. I couldn't have a better set of sisters-in-law. Thank you to my brothers-in-law, Claudy and Jean, for always having my back and being good uncles to my sons. It's much appreciated.

Thank you, Abuela, for being my superwoman when I needed one. You saved the day more times than I could count. Yo te quiero mucho! Thank you, Titi Toni and Titi Esther, for your guidance throughout my adolescence. You cared enough about me to compel me to greatness. Thank you, cousin Lou, for being the best big brother known to humankind. I've learned how to successfully navigate the streets of New York City and beyond in part because of you.

Thank you, Idris, for being my brother from another mother. Thanks for keeping me on task. Thanks to all my family and friends who asked me from time to time how the book was coming along and/or took some time to read a few chapters and give me some honest feedback. Thanks to all the individuals throughout the years who encouraged me to write a book. Thanks to the countless young people I've come into contact with who reminded me of how important it was for me to finish this book.

To my nieces, nephews, and godchildren, I love you all tremendously. Stay focused and always positive. The world will tempt you to do otherwise. To my sons, Elijah and Isaiah, I am so proud to be your father. I never thought it would be possible for someone to love an individual more than him- or herself until I met you guys. I love you both unconditionally. This one is for you!

INTRODUCTION

In 2002, I began my first job out of college at a nonprofit organization housed in Brooklyn, New York. As a program coordinator, I worked in a number of rough-around-the-edges-type public high schools with the responsibility of providing students with a series of guest speakers and a culminating college trip. The concept was brilliant. It was based upon the idea that young people need to hear inspirational stories of triumph from people who look like them to be instilled with hope and a positive outlook on their lives.

But little did I know I was slated to be the first guest speaker. I was terrified because up until that point, I had never shared specific details about my life with anyone outside of my circle. I never really saw the significance in doing so. Although I was anxious about how I would be perceived, I wrote a forty-minute presentation, stood in front of a ninth-grade class of thirty-four students, and spoke candidly about how I managed to survive despite challenging conditions presented in my life. To my surprise, the response was remarkable.

A number of students thanked me for sharing and stated that my story deeply resonated with them.

A few even asked to continue the conversation for their sake or the sake of someone they knew who was going through a particular storm and needed a bit of encouragement. I also received a few letters of gratitude that really made my heart smile. The experience left me with a mission, a charge to address a serious issue in my community and communities like it—the lack of positive black and Latino male role models. From that point forward, it was ingrained in me that young people need positive individuals who represent symbols of hope for them who they can aspire to emulate.

Since then, my life's mission has been to give back to my community by using my personal story as an example to motivate others who are dealing with real-life issues that seem intolerable. I've witnessed the positive impact that sharing stories of inspiration has on young people. I've seen firsthand the immediate change in a young person's way of thinking and doing after being exposed to personal stories of triumph. These young people realize that all is not lost. They understand that they're not alone, because there are people who have similar backgrounds, grew up in similar neighborhoods, and experienced similar circumstances, yet they have done well despite the odds stacked against them. I am a testament to the adage "Where there's a will, there's a way."

Over the years, I've presented my life story to thousands of young people in various institutions, such as colleges/universities, GED centers, vocational trade schools, elementary and middle schools, and high schools. Interestingly, I'm often asked how I did it. I'm usually asked to give explicit details on how I went from drowning to driving the boat. For a long time, I really couldn't answer that question. I realized that I couldn't answer it because it wasn't a simple answer. A combination of multiple things happened in my life that contributed to my not becoming another statistic. It's impossible for me to pinpoint one specific reason that accurately illustrates my path to success.

I wrote this book as a testament of my life, describing the many trials and tribulations I had to endure to get to where I am today. Hopefully the words penned on these pages will reach out and positively touch the lives of many. The circumstances outlined in this book and the ways in which I managed to deal with them are specific to me. Not everyone follows the same exact path to success. I encourage you to use this book as a blueprint to help you map out a path to success that is specific to you.

According to the dictionary, the definition of *unexpected* is "not expected or regarded as likely to happen." The first half of my life is directly aligned with this meaning. In the eyes of many, including myself at the time, it wasn't expected that I'd attend college and obtain a degree, live to the age of twenty-four, stay out of prison, get married and stick around until death do us part, father children and play an essential role in their lives, or find creative ways to give back to my community. It's with a tremendous amount of grace and fortitude that I incredibly defied the odds and did the unexpected.

You can too!

1

SQUARE ONE

I remember it like it was yesterday. At the impressionable age of three times three, I stand poised at the precipice of life—entangled in my thoughts like prey in a spider's silk. It's like an unforgettable beat with a catchy hook that plays over and over in my head. The horns are arranged so perfectly, like one of my favorite rap songs, Pete Rock and CL Smooth's "T.R.O.Y." It's like the aroma beaming off a porcelain plate stacked four meats high of chuletas fritas that jogs my recollection. They are vivid memories of a time not so long ago that is forever etched in my brain and impossible to erase.

The day flew by, and the darkness of the night quickly engulfed the boogie-down Bronx like a thick fog. The projects were on the verge of being consumed by the haze, but through the flickers of light from the light post, one could easily see five stories up to our apartment. It signaled the obvious. It was time for us to go to bed or "hit the bunk," as my mom would often yell. My little brother, Joseph, was always the first one to fall asleep and naturally the first one to be at the receiving end of the whipped-cream-in-the-ear prank—especially on a Friday night. For reasons unknown, I had of habit of making the lives of those who I liked a lot or loved a little slightly uncomfortable. But despite the countless Fridays I chose to flood his eardrums with whipped or shaving cream or on occasion baby powder, he was my best buddy—my partner in mischief.

While he shockingly ate spinach out of a can like Popeye, Joseph didn't like to eat much. He was always the last one to leave the dinner table. It didn't sit well with his gag reflex to see an unplucked feather or two on a chicken wing or drumstick, so on my days when I was being super greedy, I took advantage of his phobia and helped him out a little. If not, he'd sit for hours at the dinner table trying to figure out a foolproof plan of escape. Then one glorious day—one for the unofficial record books—he came up with the idea to spread the food around the plate to make it seem like he had eaten most of it. I couldn't believe it passed plate inspection (for a few weeks at least until mom caught on).

One sheep, two sheep, three sheep, four. Off to dreamland we went, and I hoped I didn't snore.

But somewhere in between a good dream and a loud snort, I woke up drenched in a cold sweat. That's what I get for watching *Friday the 13th* two days prior. It was not that I was scared or anything, but I

Anthony Perseveres

thought the smartest thing for me to do was to turn on the television. The light radiating from the tube could help me see through the pitch-black darkness that consumed my room, and maybe it would help me go back to sleep.

But as I went to lie back down on the bottom bunk, I noticed a bunch of strange shadows moving back and forth underneath my bedroom door. I also heard unfamiliar voices whispering to each other, as if they had something to hide. There was more than one person in the hallway walking to and from my uncle G's bedroom. One of them turned on the bathroom faucet in an attempt to drown out their voices, but I was two steps ahead of them. Taking a lesson out of Inspector Gadget's detective book, I put an empty drinking glass (it just so happened that I had one in my bedroom) to my bedroom wall so I could amplify the sound. I was on the case faster than it took for you to read this sentence.

Although I couldn't quite hear what they were saying, I identified the voices as coming from two women. I had a suspicious feeling about them and wanted to bust out of my bedroom and practice my WWF wrestling moves. I'd been itching for an opportunity to rip off my T-shirt like Hulk Hogan, and this seemed like a perfect time.

Almost every night I dreamt of winning a championship belt after defeating Andre the Giant with a thundering leg drop. I even created a wrestling belt out of cardboard and wore it to elementary school one day, but that's a whole other story. After contemplating if I should Hulk Hogan them or not, I decided to disregard my suspicions and fell fast asleep. Besides, there were always creepy-looking and weird-sounding people coming in and out of Uncle G's bedroom at any given time of night.

A few hours later, Saturday morning dawned. The sun was shining, summer vacation was fast approaching, and the fourth grade was soon to be nothing but a distant memory. The signature laugh of one of my favorite cartoon characters, Woody Woodpecker, echoed through the hallway from Uncle G's bedroom. The laugh triggered an immediate response in Joseph to wake up wildly without any regard for me sleeping in the bunk below—not that he ever had any regard. I could hear him wrestling with his Spider-Man sheets, trying to find the right time to spring into action.

Suddenly, with the power of Zeus embodied in a seven-year-old, he leaped from the top bunk, tapped me on the shoulder, and whispered, "Jahan, are you awake?"

"No, I'm not awake, so go back to sleep," I replied.

And with a devilish tone in his voice, he answered, "People who are asleep don't talk." It was his job as a little brother to annoy me, and he did it so well.

He was still hyper from the intense "shoe fight" we'd had with Uncle G the night before. It was our unique way of bonding. We connected through extreme physical acts of possible injury. Joseph and I worked as a team, constructing couch pillow barricades and shoe box catapults, and demonstrated rapid shoe fire. Joseph was looking for a rematch as he bent down and grabbed a size ten shell-top Adidas and quickly made his way to Uncle G's bedroom to continue the onslaught. He slipped and slid his way to the bedroom on account of his footie pajamas on our linoleum tile floors.

"Wake up, Uncle G! I bet you can't block this one!" Joseph shouted.

There was a deafening silence. This seemed strange to Joseph because we all knew that Uncle G would wake up from hearing the sound of a pin drop in the next room or a feather dusting a ceiling fan, so he sensed that something was wrong. Joseph superhero Flash bolted back to our bedroom and yelled, "Jahan, something's wrong with Uncle G."

This is worth an investigation, I thought. I entered my uncle's bedroom and immediately felt a cool breeze in the air. The breeze made the hair on the back of my neck stand up like a soldier at attention. I surveyed the room and realized it was a little messier than usual, with empty beer bottles and balled up paper all over the floor.

I also noticed that he wasn't wearing much clothing but a pair of white Fruit of the Loom underwear and a multicolored sheet wrapped around his legs. I attempted to wake him by shaking him and yelling, "Uncle G, Uncle G!" I was somewhat familiar with death and dying from watching inappropriate movies not suited for young eyes and minds, so I immediately thought he was gone.

Time seemed to stand still as I dropped to my knees and cried until my eyes were swollen and sensitive to touch. The tears fell to the floor and sounded like thunder. Then, in a lightning flash, I was back to reality. Looking in the floor-length mirror, I saw that my face resembled any boxer who dared to fight Mike Tyson in his prime. I somehow found the strength to stand up. I pulled Uncle G's underwear further to his waist as if to make sure he looked more presentable. I didn't want anyone to see my uncle in this condition. By this time, Joseph had joined me in my waterworks session. My mom woke up from all the noise we were making and realized what had happened. She checked his pulse and dialed 911, and ever since then, my life hasn't been the same.

Square one.

Uncle G didn't stand on street corners like most present-day drug dealers. He sold crack cocaine straight out of our apartment, so crackheads and every Tom, Dick, and Jerome banged on our door at any time of day or night, whether it was noon on a Saturday or three o'clock on a Monday morning. Like clockwork almost every thirty minutes throughout an entire twenty-four-hour period, someone would bang on our door for drugs. For fun, sort of, Joseph and I would place bets on the next time someone would knock. We weren't supposed to be up past nine o'clock, but who could really sleep in Grand Central Station?

"I bet you five Now and Laters and two Sour Powers someone will knock at midnight," Joseph said.

"Bet," I answered while at the same time securing it with the traditional pinky and thumb bump.

And before I knew it, "Bang, bang, bang!" A knock at the door. "Who is it?" I shouted.

"It's me," an unfamiliar voice on the other side of the door responded.

"Me who?" As if when they said their name I'd know who it was.

But it really didn't matter who it was because I checked the time and the clock read midnight. I had lost the bet. "It didn't count because I had my fingers crossed," I told Joseph.

"Yeah right, don't give me that stuff. You lost fair and square," Joseph replied.

He was right, but that was the last time I ever put my candy on the line. Nothing was worth me losing a Sour Power or some strawberry Now & Laters over. There were many times (more than I care to admit) when I answered and opened the door for someone who wanted to buy drugs. It was the norm. Not that I had a choice in the matter, but I did it without any regard for my own safety. I put my life and the lives of my family members in jeopardy each time I let someone in because I was in the middle of individuals strung out on drugs and those who sold it, which was a bad combination.

Yet I thought my uncle G was the coolest guy on the face of our blue planet. He fell asleep each night with a stocking cap on his head to keep the waves in his hair spinning like the spokes on my BMX bike. His pockets were always full of money, and he entertained pretty women regularly. He was an avid Run DMC fan, so he wore a big gold chain, Cazal designer frames, sheepskin coats, Kangol hats, and Adidas sneakers with the fat shoelaces. Every now and then I'd gain access to his closet (without permission, of course) and try something on and pretend to be him.

"I want you to walk this way," I would sing in front of the mirror, repeating the lyrics to one of his favorite rap songs with a ditty bop stride. Run DMC used to be on constant rotation and on full blast back then.

But what made him even cooler was the fact that he loved all his nieces and nephews like we were his own children and protected us like a mother bear and its cubs. If any of us had a problem with anyone in the neighborhood or at school, he would go out of his way to solve it. Even though he only stood five-foot-five and weighed well over two hundred pounds, he possessed the power of an ox and the speed of a cheetah. As a child growing up, I heard many stories of Uncle G "Carl Lewising" people half his weight with style and grace and "Mike Tysoning" men a foot taller than he was. Some instances I witnessed firsthand.

He was the closest thing I knew to having a male figure in my life who took a vested interest in me. I was his number-one fan. I looked up to him as a father figure, especially since my biological sperm donor was MIA.

Never did I imagine that Uncle G would leave me without saying good-bye. But it was something he had no control over. The autopsy revealed that he used a variety of illegal drugs, namely heroin and cocaine. And due to the drugs in his system combined with his obesity, he had a heart attack and died in his sleep. But I always wondered if the two women knew of something that could've prevented his death and if they left the apartment before or after he died. Maybe that's what all the whispering and sneaky behavior were about. I guess I'll never really know the truth behind that night.

He was only twenty-four years old—a sad end to another young man who expired way before his time. Ironically, another one of my uncles (his older brother) also died at the age of twenty-four a few years prior. There seemed to be a sinister pattern here, I thought. I hoped I could disrupt death's pattern and make it past twenty-four years old.

After my mom gave birth to a boy and he died in his sleep in that same room at nine months old, I was afraid to enter it. It was designated the "death room," and none of my brothers and sisters wanted to set one foot in there. One too many people died within its four walls, and we weren't interested in being the third or fourth victims. It was as if the room was cursed with an evil spirit that was hungry for souls. But only time would tell if the "death room" would call again. Until then, we made sure to steer clear of it.

A year prior to Uncle G's death, my mom moved my two siblings and me to the projects to live with *mi abuela* (my grandmother). My uncles, G and Larry, shared a bedroom directly across from my grandmother's bedroom. It was a two-bedroom apartment that was now occupied by seven people. The Brady Bunch had nothing on us—minus the big, expensive house, maid, and father, that is. It was supposed to be a temporary living arrangement, so we set up camp in the living room and slept on the pull-out couch bed.

The projects we lived in is located in the northeast section of the Bronx and is classified as the third-largest housing projects in New York City. There were many high-rise buildings that rose either three or fourteen stories tall and stretched for miles throughout the complex. There were pockets of well-manicured grass and trees that surrounded the building we lived in. Black gates outlined the places that were highly suggested to be off limits to residents. But we didn't take suggestions well. In front of the building we lived in was a miniature park with a slide and monkey bars made of wood and metal. The park lasted for a short while because some girl decided to toss everything but the kitchen sink out the window. From ten stories up, with pinpoint accuracy, she hit a few people with her mother's red pocketbook, a left tennis shoe, and a china dinner plate.

The larger parks within the projects had carefully painted basketball courts that provided great opportunities for kids to hone their skills, aspiring to be the next Air Jordan or Larry Bird. If only the rims could stay on long enough. But I wasn't the greatest basketball player. The ball never seemed to find the inside of the hoop often enough for me to claim the rights to be an MVP. So instead, I enjoyed flipping on dirty mattresses in the spring, turning the fire hydrant on full blast in the summer, and playing tackle football in the snow in the winter.

I considered myself to be a sweet, lovable, black Puerto Rican kid who occasionally had some mean tendencies. I tended to hide my brother's action figures, which he loved so much, just because I thought it was fun to watch him look for them in a frantic frenzy. I tended to rearrange my sister Jenny's Barbie dolls by replacing the heads with scary-looking troll heads and painting the faces with any color permanent marker I could find.

I had not-so-curly hair and the male version of Olive Oyl legs. My mom was a bit taller than one of the seven dwarfs, and I guessed my biological sperm donor wasn't much taller than her because I was kind of short for my age. I was three-and-a-half-feet-nothing tall. I hated size place order. I was never the first standing in the front of a line, but I was usually number two or three. I might as well have been the first.

But I was a typical kid with big hopes and even bigger dreams. I wished to be an astronaut like Neil Armstrong. I imagined exploring deep space, hopping from planet to planet, collecting stars in a glass jar like I collected lightning bugs. Or I pictured being a paleontologist, leading mass expeditions to discover new species of dinosaurs. And along the way, I would name a few dinosaurs after me. There was something about exploring the realms of the "unknown" that really piqued my interest and fascinated me. I was also intrigued by nature. I'd sit glued in front of the television, watching channel 13 nature shows with extreme enthusiasm.

I couldn't swim to save my life. Yeah, that's typical. I was the only nine-year-old boy in the pool with arm floats holding on to a big doughnut tube with a "you can only pry it from my hands when I'm dead" grip. The concept of putting my head underwater where there was literally no oxygen didn't sit well with my lungs. And it didn't help that I was freakishly terrified of sharks, especially great white sharks. As a consequence, with every courageous dip I took at the local beach or pool, I'd hear "the shark is coming to eat me" theme from the movie *Jaws*. I really needed to stop watching those scary movies.

By the time I was thirteen years old, I learned how to ride a two-wheeler—a lot older than most kids. So typical. My older cousin Rico took me under his wing and tried his best to school me. I had a silver and black BMX bike that quenched my thirst for a fast burst. But the problem was that I needed speed like I needed a broken leg. As I sped down Devil's Hill, without a helmet or protective gear, a little shaky in the knowledge of how to steer away from objects, I saw a faint dark image a few feet ahead of me. I tried vigorously to avoid it, but instead I was somehow magnetically attracted to it. Boom! Who put that black gate there? The next time I was out playing crash test dummy, I made it my business not to smash into the same gate. Instead, I slammed into the gate right next to it. My hand-eye coordination was grossly undeveloped.

The community we lived in was occupied by thousands of Latino and African American families that were classified as poor. It was an underserved neighborhood that lacked resources but had an abundance of other things surrounding its borders. There were stores that claimed to sell everything for ninety-nine cents, but when you went in to purchase an item, the price jumped to $2.58. The sign outside should've read, "Some items sold for ninety-nine cents but not everything store." Also, liquor stores were conveniently situated on the corner of every block. Absolutely every single block had a liquor store at the corner of it.

The most affordable foods were the ones that could kill you if you ate them enough. You could buy a whole meal for three dollars at the local fried chicken with a bucket of grease. A slow death by way of fried gizzard wasn't uncommon. It almost seemed as if there were special forces at work trying to keep us fat and drunk. Now why would someone want to keep us overweight and intoxicated? I could write a whole other book based on that question, but for now let's get back to the story.

When we arrived at the projects, we were unfortunately about to enter the crack cocaine epidemic of the '80s and '90s that infiltrated and ransacked many communities of color. It tore apart thousands of families and devastated whole communities like the bubonic plague. The crack cocaine era led to many residences being designated as crack houses. They were easy to identify because if you walked into an apartment, it had little to no furniture and spewed a noxious smell that was a mixture between burnt rubber and gasoline—a smell that evasively attached itself to my nostrils like a blood-sucking parasite. It was a smell that haunted my dreams—a smell I could recognize to this day.

Anthony Perseveres

2

STICKS AND STONES

Growing up, I often viewed life through dark and weary eyes. The world and the people in it represented objects of varied degrees of strength as with sticks and stones. I came in contact with many individuals who were weak and a few who were strong and functioned to only prey on the weak. Sticks can snap with enough pressure applied, and stones can crack if thrown against the pavement enough times with enough force. I frequently wondered if I was a stick or a stone. When would I snap or crack?

After the untimely death of Uncle G, mom became severely depressed, and it seemed as if a part of her (some of the good parts) died with him. For the next few months, she mourned his death, crying most nights for hours upon hours until her tear ducts dried up or her knees became swollen, whichever came first. I used to hear her in the back bedroom wailing, asking Jehovah why he took Uncle G away from her so soon. And as a young boy at the age of nine,

I watched as my mom slowly deteriorated into a shell of a woman who had once stood strong. She found it extremely difficult to cope with her little brother passing away. In her mind, it seemed she had lost someone who fully understood her pain and whose love was unconditional.

They had a love-hate relationship. If they got into a heated discussion on any particular night, by the morning, all was forgotten, as if nothing had ever occurred. And if anyone dared to get in between them, they had better be prepared to feel the wrath of Khan. Innocent bystanders in the midst of an altercation were far from safe. You might very well have both of them at your throat before you could even guess how you initially got involved. Blood was definitely thicker than water in their book.

And due to the loss of that bond, she attempted to fill the void through a substance. She would, as I called it at the time, "be on a mission." This meant like a soldier at war, she would be determined to complete her mission objective—to obtain the rock. It was not the kind of rock that shines but the one that dulls the spirit and destroys the soul. It was the rock that swept in and flooded my neighborhood and others similar to it like Hurricane Katrina—the rock that killed thousands of blacks and Latinos without a warning, with no remorse, and with no sign of rescue in sight. The rock was unaffectionately known as crack cocaine.

Anthony Perseveres

When she was on a mission, she took on a whole new persona. It was like watching Dr. Jekyll transform into Mr. Hyde. And crack cocaine was the formula that changed her into something unimaginable. It altered her attitude toward herself. Mom always paid close attention to detail, especially when it came to her outward appearance. She learned at a very early age how to style her own hair. But when she was on a mission, she didn't care about how she dressed or how her hair looked. I remember how her long black hair would be twisted and knotted. And her clothes didn't fit well on her five-foot-two frame, with shirts slightly off the shoulder and pants unbuckled and droopy. She was virtually unrecognizable as her eyes laid low and sunk into the back of her head. Her dark complexion appeared pale, almost ghostlike. Additionally, she developed a condition that made her pinky twitch on the right side of her hand. Hence, my siblings and I all knew when mom was on a mission. The pinky twitch was a dead giveaway that sent chills through our spines and anxiety into our hearts.

Speaking of Tingling Sensations

In today's society, spanking a child is frowned upon. But back in the day, it was as common as the common cold. We received our fair share of whippings like most children did for misbehaving. It wasn't one of those "go outside and get the switch" kind of situations, but it was a whipping nonetheless. There was something special about how we were disciplined and how we tried to evade it. In an intense moment, Joseph and I would run into our bedrooms and hide under the bed to avoid a butt whipping. Or we would cover ourselves with a thick quilt to soften the blows to our backsides. Unluckily for us, mom had every butt-whipping instrument at her disposal and knew how to adjust to challenging circumstances rather nicely.

She'd poke a broomstick under the bed with one hand and with the other hand pull the blankets back to expose our tender young flesh. I tried my best to hide all the leather belts and break the plastic clothing hangers (her favorite weapons of choice) in advance because I knew a spanking was just around the corner. The occasional chancleta reared its ugly sole every now and then. I always got into trouble for doing something mischievous—like the time I tricked Joseph into standing still on the bed so I could practice my kung fu kick. "Don't worry," I reassured him as he slowly stood up and looked behind his shoulder as if calling for help.

"You think I would really hurt you?" I asked.

"Yes!" he said.

I ended up knocking him two feet off the bed. He got a knot on the side of his head the size of a golf ball. I put my hand over his mouth to try and muffle the screams. But it didn't work. You could guess what I got for pretending to be a kung fu master. Have you ever gotten smacked in your head and felt it in your stomach or gotten a pinch twist in your arm and felt it throughout your body? I used to think parents attended "The Art of Butt Whipping" class in order to master the technique. I actually thought my mom taught the class.

"Now what you have to do, ladies and gentlemen, is find the fleshly part of your child's body," mom would instruct with a stern look on her face.

"For example," she would say as she modeled for the parents in attendance with her right arm held high, "a perfect spot for twisting is the flabby part of the arm between the hand and elbow. It's important that you get into a sturdy stance to balance yourself as you grab hold of it with your thumb and index fingers. Once positioned in place, you need to give it a three hundred sixty–degree turn. This will allow for maximum pressure to be applied and the pain receptors to be properly stimulated."

Mom also had a stare that could crack glass like an opera singer. You know, the type of stare that spoke a thousand words without a person uttering a single word? She had the "don't play with me or I'll blankety blank you up" stare. Also, she mastered the "you can play with me now but when we get home your butt is mine" look. She was a real tough cookie, like the ones left out in the open after four days. But in the kitchen, she had a delicate, magical touch. Merlin the Great would've been envious. Her *arroz con gandules* was absolutely something to die for. She committed all her recipes to memory—a true master chef without the professional training.

I grew up in a single-parent household where my mom took care of my four younger siblings (three additional siblings were eventually born) and me to the best of her ability. She was a strong black Latina who played a dual role as a mom and dad. And as a young mother at the age of nineteen, she had to quickly learn how to take care of me without much support from family or my biological sperm donor.

And due to the fact that she dropped out of high school in the tenth grade, she was headed for a difficult journey without an education. Yet she was resourceful and managed to utilize her street smarts to secure some jobs and received public assistance from the government. Even though most of my friends received some form of government assistance, I was embarrassed to admit to anyone that I was on welfare. The Eddie Murphys and Martin Lawrences of the world weren't going to make me the butt of their jokes. I liked to eat but not at the cost of losing some cool points. I did my best to hide the fact that we were being helped by the government.

I'd walk into a store with mom and felt like all eyes were focused on me—like everyone in the store knew that I had a pocket full of food stamps. My mission was to gather all the items we wanted to buy and look for a line that had the least amount of people. The hope was that I didn't bump into anyone I knew. My covert operation to get the goods and go never quite worked out how I imagined.

"Jahan, bring me the food stamps I gave you to buy this food," mom would shout, making sure that everyone in the store heard and saw that she was talking to me.

"Yeah you, with the blue shirt and blond-streaked flattop, bring me the food stamps from out of your pocket."

And as I cringed and wished that I could just disappear, I slowly reached into my pocket and handed her a bundle of food stamps.

"You don't like it until I come home with the Pop Tarts and Cap'n Crunch cereal I bought with it," she would joke. She always knew the right words to say to make me feel so good inside.

I understood later on in life that she was trying to make a point—to not be ashamed about what you have now in order to appreciate what you'll get later. But I despised food stamps and walking into a supermarket to purchase items with red and blue money—I mean a stack of red and blue money that you had to take your time removing from a booklet. The fancy EBT debit cards that exist today were decades away from creation.

It was like playing Monopoly but in real life. However, unlike the game, we didn't have the option to buy prime real estate, yet mom managed to keep a roof above our heads, clothes on our backs, and food in our stomachs. And if you wanted to keep the food fresh and pest free, you had to store it in sealed canisters or else the brown brothers (roaches) would invade the territory and lay waste to the land. Their numbers counted somewhere in the hundreds, perhaps in the thousands. The fastest thing on six legs, they came like thieves in the night, eating everything in their path. They are masters at being elusive and difficult to kill because they multiply faster than you can spray them. Afraid of the light, they scamper and hide to avoid it. That's just how it was living in the PJs. Anything left out in the open was fair game—and not just for the roaches.

On the first and fifteenth of each month, I had to stand in a long line that stretched around the corner to get a block of cheese (it measured two feet and weighed five pounds) that we had to cut with a butcher knife, stuck to the roof of our mouths, and lasted for what seemed like forever. And I never cut the cheese correctly, but who did? There wasn't a cutting guide that said cut this amount, so I made the thickest cheese sandwiches, with one side always bigger than the other. Try to imagine a two-by-four stuck between two pieces of bread. Not a pretty sight. I always wondered how they made the cheese blocks. Did they pour melted cheese into molds like cement and let it cool and harden overnight?

Nonetheless, to make matters worse, because my vision wasn't the clearest, I had to wear prescription coke-bottle glasses. And being a child on welfare meant that there were only a select few generic frames to choose from. It was either the frames in glass case number one or the frames in glass case number one. I swore that's what the world's plastic recycled into: eyeglasses for poor kids. I probably wore a few frisbees and water cooler bottles in my day.

With my right hand placed on a stack of Bibles, I swear I lost each and every pair of glasses by mistake.

I mistakenly sat on my first pair of glasses, accidentally threw the second pair out the window, and not deliberately left my third pair on a bus. It really didn't matter that I looked like Mr. Magoo (a cartoon about a nearly blind detective who managed to solve crimes despite his disability) when I wore them. I appreciated the time mom took to ensure my popularity in school was equivalent to Steve Urkel's. Possibly being labeled four eyes had absolutely nothing to do with me losing them.

Sticks and stones.

But without them, I might as well have been using bat radar to find my way around or to identify people. Faces appeared fuzzy from a distance. I couldn't tell if I walked by someone I knew or Apollonia from the movie *Purple Rain*. She was like Halle Berry in the mid-'80s. Oh how I wanted to meet Ms. Apollonia and have her ride on the back of my motorcycle like she did with Prince in the movie. It was a childhood fantasy I immediately dismissed after I gave up guitar lessons.

Go figure.

Needless to say, I had poor vision. Therefore, I wore my government-issues until I was old enough to work and afford what I thought was a good pair of eyeglasses. Nevertheless, my mom and abuela managed to buy me some name-brand clothing and high-quality footwear for school. That's one thing about some Latino families. We make sure that we look good regardless of what our house looks like or if our bills are paid. The lights may be off, but we'll go into a department store and pay $150 for a pair of Air Jordans. We can only receive incoming phone calls, but our hair is flowing in the wind and our nails are gleaming in the sun. We are financially challenged but want to give off the impression that we pop champagne and dine on caviar regularly.

Sorry if I'm being too real, but I must be true to this story. Actually, I'm not sorry. I take that back. More often than not, our priorities are in the wrong place, so we make adjustments in our lives in an attempt to fit a certain image. The media tells us to behave, speak, and look a particular way to be accepted by society, and we make it our business to accommodate. I'm not saying that there's something wrong with someone wanting to dress nice, but your rent shouldn't go unpaid because of it.

What types of messages are we sending our young people if we continue to hold material things in such high regard? We are telling them that it's more important for them to look good rather than to take care of their responsibilities. The kinds of sacrifices we must make should only be made for the sake of what society deems appropriate. We really need to reevaluate our lives and pay closer attention to the things that are truly valuable—our young people. Please take a minute to reflect on that.

Joseph and I attended a nearby elementary school that was only four blocks away from our home. I swear those four blocks felt like four miles when I was constantly on a lookout to avoid trouble. We were like zebras on the African plains, constantly aware of our surroundings and keeping a watchful eye out for predators.

On the first block, the streets were littered with broken glass and paper like the day after a parade. We stayed close together so the wolves couldn't separate us. They could smell fear, so we had to act tough and look into their eyes but not long enough to look like we wanted trouble.

On the second block, we saw a drug addict or two, maybe three. Some people were screaming out their windows, "Man, you don't know me!" There were a bunch of dudes standing in front of some buildings, just standing around as if they were waiting or a bus or for an unsuspecting kid to be off his or her guard.

The third block was a hazardous street intersection where cars whizzed by and many kids were injured. Across the street, students from a high school were on the field practicing for their next football game. And not too far away from the field, troublemakers swarmed the area like bees to something sweet. Some kids were being harassed to join a team but not for sports or anything fun.

The fourth block signaled that we were in for the home stretch. The school was just a stone's throw away. I could see the crossing guard with salt-and-pepper hair who'd been making sure students could get safely across the streets for the past twenty years. And as we entered the school building, there was a sigh of relief. We made it. Now we had to just hope we could make it back home without a scratch.

Mom picked us up from school only on occasion. Thank Jehovah. She was a bit too paranoid. Holding her hand as a fifth grader was probably not the best way for me to be considered one of the cool kids. Totally uncool. On the days we walked home by ourselves, we took alternate routes, stayed close to groups of other kids going our way, and made sure we didn't stop to talk to anyone. Don't ask us for directions, what time it was, or what the math homework was for Ms. Smith's class because we didn't stop to talk to anyone and I mean no one.

Safety first.

Anthony Perseveres

And for valid reasons. We lived in a dangerous neighborhood. There were many individuals (males in particular) on just about every corner or block who were members of gangs or crews. I witnessed countless acts of violence against my peers and always wondered when it would be my turn to be a victim. I believed it was only a matter of time before they got to me, so I was always on red alert. I was prepared to respond to any situation to protect myself or my family. And as the eldest sibling/man of the house, I was determined to make sure my family was safe.

We fell asleep most nights to the sound of gunshots and woke up in the morning wondering if we were going to make it through the day in one piece. And each shot that blared out put me in a state of shock because I often imagined who felt the bullet. Was it an innocent person walking down the street or a grandmother sitting in her living room watching *Jeopardy*?

But there were some days when it was so quiet that I could hear a person's footsteps outside of my fifth-floor window. Or I could hear a young man's rhyme line for line on how he wanted to live life free from crime. Ironically, the quiet days seemed to be the most unusual. I became so accustomed to the bang-bang, shoot 'em up style lullaby that what should have been the norm (peace and quiet) was now odd and out of place.

3

UP IN SMOKE

Like an out-of-whack spinning compass, countless bodies were stretched out in all directions. They were all just lying there lifeless, energy depleted and on the negative side. It was five times below the zero. Someone sucked the life right out of them like a vacuum and left them alone to die a slow, miserable death. The last breath they inhaled caressed their lungs and flowed through their bloodstream many moments ago. They were so skinny that I could see right through them, almost invisible. Their white tops were whiter than a polar bear's coat, than eggshells, than freshly fallen snow. My mind began to play tricks on me like the Geto Boys on All Hollow's Eve. I could hear them laughing, a bad guy in a movie who has an evil plot to destroy the good guy kind of laugh. If there's a word for being beyond horrified, I was it.

The first time I saw a glass pipe and empty crack vials lying on the living room table, my heart skipped a beat like a scratched-up

CD. But I wasn't in love. I was more in hate. At first glance, I didn't want my mind to believe what my eyes had just seen. I didn't want to believe that my mom was a drug addict, mainly because I was afraid. Most people who abused drugs lived rather short lives—about three feet, two inches' worth of a life. They usually died because of a drug overdose or an unpaid IOU. A debt of about ten to twenty dollars was enough to take a life.

But not this life.

I was scared to confront it, but I picked up the glass pipe and examined it like a doctor preparing for surgery. I stared into the eye of the enemy and saw that the tip of it was black. It had something stuck in the middle of it that looked like a broken piece of chalk. And right beside it was a twenty-five-cent plastic bottle (quarter water) filled halfway with water and a straw-sized hole in the center of it.

"So we finally meet at last, Mr. Crack," I scoffed. "You don't look so tough. I thought that you'd be much bigger."

"Looks are deceiving, young man," he replied. "Don't be fooled by my small stature. I've managed to single-handedly bring down giants among men. My reputation is well known."

Because I watched movies like *New Jack City*, I knew that the plastic bottle and glass pipe were used to smoke crack, so I got rid of them by tossing them down the incinerator.

"May you burn in the fiery depths of heck. The devil can have you back!" I screamed.

Up in smoke.

My anxieties didn't allow me to sleep well that night. I stood awake until dawn staring through the black safety bars on my window. I looked up toward the sky and desperately tried to find a star through all the smog. It would've served as a sign that things would get better. I just had to find one. The polluted city haze was dark, thick, and unrelenting. But just when I was about to abandon my search, a flicker of light sparked behind a cloud shaped like a turkey. It was like the spark you see when you first try to start a lighter. And that's what the cloud looked like to me—a turkey. Maybe I was hungry. Hungry for solutions is more like it.

I tried my best to think of a plan to help mom with her addiction. There had to be a way for her to get better. All I could do was pray on it—so I did. I prayed upon a star to the Alpha and Omega. The next morning, I mustered up enough courage to ask her directly if she was smoking crack. Before my discovery, although the pinky twitch was a dead giveaway, I had never officially seen her smoking crack or had any physical evidence. She denied using the pipe and said it belonged to a friend, but I didn't believe her. And for good reason—there were too many examples of extreme situations for me to believe otherwise.

Like the one Christmas that was deemed the worst holiday ever.

Like the Grinch slapped a little girl in Whoville bad. Like Scrooge took Tiny Tim's wooden walking stick and sold it on the street for $1.15 bad. Mom performed a Miracle on 229th Street and bought us a whole bunch of gifts. I thought she must've hit a number, found a pot of gold at the end of a rainbow, had a secret diamond mine, or struck black gold. It was like Santa Claus had left his big red bag behind by mistake or got jacked for it on purpose. Either way, we felt like the Cosby kids for a moment—but only for a moment.

I wasn't really sure where she got all the money to buy everything, but as a kid, I was only concerned about what was underneath the Christmas tree and behind the wrapping paper. My jaw dropped a couple of times and bounced on the linoleum floor like one of those small rubber balls as I unwrapped, with great force and vigor, a state-of-the-art stereo system, a Walkman, a triple fat goose coat, some jewelry, and a pair of boots. Now I understand that most of the things I just mentioned are foreign to many of you and no longer exist, but trust me, it was a big deal. My brother Joseph was especially pleased to receive a Walkman for Christmas because he wanted to listen to his Michael Jackson *Bad* tape. He fell asleep that night with the headphones taped to his ears.

Joseph was infatuated with Michael Jackson. It was like he came straight out of a Pepsi commercial, minus the combustible Jerry curls, superb dance skills, fading skin complexion, pet monkey, and deep pockets. He'd listen to his music all day and night, mimicking his every mannerism. With his silver-gloved hand in a place that's classified as private, doing his best rendition of the moonwalk, he'd shout, "You know I'm bad, I'm bad, you know it." And being the great big brother that I was, I would boo him off the stage and yell, "You can't sing, man! Get your light-skinned, curly-haired butt out of here!"

He even had a Michael Jackson–style leather jacket that he wore frequently, especially when company came over and he wanted to impersonate the king of pop. But when he wasn't on stage, his favorite show to watch was wrestling. No one was able to pull him away from the television set when Hulk Hogan or the Ultimate Warrior was in the ring. He even had a miniature wrestling ring and a few wrestling men that his uncle bought him one Christmas. I remember him announcing royal rumbles and perfectly imitating the voices of each character. He took it very seriously. And I was serious about hiding them. From time to time, Joseph also found a place to hide of his own.

He absolutely adored his grandparents on his father's side. If my mom disciplined him for something he did wrong, nine times out of ten, he'd sneak out of the house and walk all the way to their apartment in the South Bronx—almost seventy blocks! It was seventy blocks through the late-'80s version of the Big Apple, which was a

Anthony Perseveres

much grungier and more rotten-to-the-core city than it is today. He somehow managed to navigate through all the perils like Indiana Jones did in all of his movies but without the leather bullwhip, cool fedora, and catchy catchphrases.

He loved them so much that he spent almost every weekend with them. I really didn't understand why Joseph wanted to leave us so much. I even resented it to the point where I felt like he loved them more than us. As I grew older, I understood that his grandparents' house was a mental escape from all the drama that played out in our apartment. Plus he had a lot more freedom to go outside (physical escape) and roam the streets whenever he wanted, which was an added benefit. But with great freedom comes great responsibility. And if you disrespect that freedom, it'll have lasting consequences— consequences that Joseph would eventually be faced with.

Take a mental note.

Sometimes we need to escape from a place that's negative and find a more suitable place of positivity. If you're constantly being exposed to things that are negative, it'll weigh heavy on your spirit, which could lead to severe depression and other things. Don't be afraid, for the sake of your own sanity, to venture off to new places that present better opportunities for you. Now, file that away in your memory bank. Hopefully you'll never need it. That Christmas, I couldn't wait to go to school and show off my new boots, coat, and gold ring to all my friends. It was like precious manna had rained down in the projects and not just on Moses and his people in the wilderness.

I think we all did this as kids (or if you're a kid reading this, you probably do this now) when we got new stuff—or maybe it was just me. Probably not. I tried everything on at least three different times to get a good idea of the best combinations. I put my boots on with the ring, the coat with my boots, and then I tried all three on at the same time.

Perfecto!

I paraded around the room like a runway model, polishing the ring and dusting off the boots every thirty seconds. Not that they needed dusting and polishing but … I was so overjoyed that I almost fell asleep with my coat, boots, and ring on. And I woke up every hour or so to check to see if the boots were still in the box. Ridiculousness times infinity. I thought I was super-duper, Missy Elliott fly.

All the girls are going to love me in this coat, I conceitedly thought. *Everybody's going to be sweating me. I'm the man, I'm the man. Yeah, you know, yeah, you know, I'm the man.*

Don't judge me. We all have a happy song.

The shock and awe eventually wore off, and we counted Zs with big smiles on our faces and contentment in our hearts. But those smiles quickly turned upside down when the sun's rays illuminated

Anthony Perseveres

the entire apartment and uncovered a troubling fact. We awoke, crust still stuck in the corner of our eyes, to an empty house. All the electronic items, along with my gold ring, were gone. The headphones were snatched right out of Joseph's ears. Mom had an "everything must go" sale at three in the morning. I guess it was fun while it lasted. We cried our eyes out until we were in need of an IV for dehydration. It was situations like this that continued to rally my suspicions, suspicions, suspicions.

On the contrary …

As I sit here writing this book about my life and all the marvelous stuff in it, my mind steadily drifts to happier times and occasions that put a smile on my face and joy in my heart. But I must confess, I searched my memory bank for months trying to locate the happy file. It seemed so much easier for me to remember the not-so-great times than it was to remember the good. I finally pulled something out that was deep down in my mind, and I couldn't believe that I almost forgot to mention it. Pardon my brief pause from the dreary, as there were some sporadic glimmers of light deep down in the abyss.

When I was around seven to about nine years old, my family and I visited my titi Carmen (my grandmother's sister) and uncle Jose during the holidays. They lived in a beautiful two-family house in the Bronx that had apple and peach trees and a shaggy dog named Striker. Striker was much bigger than I was but always greeted me with a friendly wag of the tail, low-level bark, and lick to the face. I loved that dog. I never really grew up with a pet. Actually, I never grew up with a pet that lasted longer than six months. We just didn't have the patience and the knowhow to properly care for an animal. During Christmas, the entire house was decked out in festive decorations, from the antique ornaments hanging from the ceiling to the six-foot pine tree surrounded by gifts in the corner of the living room. And every kid in the house who came to visit had a present with his or her name on it under that tree. As soon as I entered the house, I made sure I located my gift and shook it a few times to try and figure out what was inside. It was probably the only time during the year I wished I had X-ray vision. And when the clock struck midnight, everyone gathered by the Christmas tree and exchanged gifts. It was a scene straight out of your favorite Christmas movie.

The smell of yellow rice and beans, sweet plantains, and chicken swept through the house. It brought sweet pleasure to our nostrils and eventually sustenance to our stomachs. Titi Carmen was a chef at heart. She knew how to throw down in the kitchen. A petite woman, she stood a little over four feet, eleven inches but was a towering figure in my eyes. She called me by my nickname, Jahnito, which meant little Jahan in Spanglish. She was such a gracious host and a pleasant person to be around. I called her at least a 102 times when I was in the hospital ill from spinal meningitis. Maybe I called her so many times because I had an extreme comfort level with her or maybe because it was the only phone number I could easily remember. I think it was because of her soothing voice and willingness to listen.

The music of Nat King Cole singing a popular tune or a famous doo wop group remixing a Christmas song set the holiday tone. The children's music selection was limited. Actually, it didn't exist. We had no choice but to listen to "In the Still of the Night" and "Feliz Navidad" a hundred times over or until the record skipped, whatever came first.

But I liked old-school music because mom would play oldies but goodies all night long as loud as the stereo volume could possibly go. It was an essential part of her routine when she cleaned up the house, reminisced about the good ol' days, or had a little bit too much to drink. I grew up listening to Barry White, the O'Jays, Marvin Gaye, and Luther Vandross, just to name a few. By the time I was nine years old, I knew the words to many old-school rhythm and blues songs and sang along to them like karaoke.

For entertainment, all the adults sat in the dining room at a large table to play card games for the fun of taking each other's money. They would play cards for hours as the children ran around the house and in the backyard playing hide and go seek. Intrigued by the display, I used to sit on my mother or abuela's lap and asked them how to play. The usual response was "Maybe when you grow up." But I noticed that the relatives who had tall stacks of quarters, nickels, and dimes in front of them were more willing to teach me than those who were penny pinching. Or sometimes, as short as I was, I'd approach the table and look over it, with my eyes barely clearing the edge, and just watch everyone play. Peeking into their hands, I'd try to guess what card they'd play next. Sometimes I got it right, but most of the time I was far from guessing correctly.

Uncle Jose was a hardworking New York City transit worker. He stood about six feet tall, had a thick mustache, and orchestrated the hair comb-over. He was the type of guy who would slip you a twenty-dollar bill just because it was the cool thing to do. Or maybe he thought that's what uncles are supposed to do for their nephews because without fail, every single time we visited, he'd call me to the room or in the hallway and give me some money. But he didn't just call me into the room. It was a discreet kind of a "psssst come over here" call. He'd act like he was giving me top-secret information and the message would self-destruct. Looking in all directions to make sure no one was around, he'd reach into his pocket and pull out a twenty-dollar bill.

"Put it in your pocket, Jahnito," he would say. "Don't tell anyone I gave it to you."

Even when I became a young adult, Uncle Jose made it his business to share the wealth. Sadly, within months of my uncle G's death, Titi Carmen passed away. It was the end of a golden era. Up

Anthony Perseveres

in smoke! I guess all good things must come to an end. My uncle Jose soon remarried, and I seldom got to see him. The special thing about my titi Carmen and uncle Jose was the fact that they provided the entire family with an outlet to get together. They also exhibited a hospitality and genuine love for family togetherness that was and still is unmatched. So my Christmases weren't all bad.

Growing up, my mother was very strict—a notch or two below Cinderella's stepsisters strict. Like Q-tips and cups of soapy water scrubbing the floors on my knees strict. No, not that strict.

Toothbrushes and buckets instead.

Negative thoughts seemed to invade her mind, like how we stormed the beaches of Normandy, when it came to the safety of her children. We were treated like newly hatched tadpoles swimming in a swamp full of hungry alligators. She'd hardly ever allow us to go outside and play for fear that something terrible would befall us. It was as if the sky would literally fall, planets collide, and the universe turn upside down once we stepped foot outside.

Even if I asked to play outside in front of the building, my request (which turned into begging on my knees) was usually denied. Yes, it was dangerous to play outside because of all the violence, but I didn't want to be held hostage in my own home. I guess her anxieties stemmed from the play-by-play reminiscing she would narrate for us of her childhood growing up in an unsafe environment. She would give us a vivid account of her childhood, especially when she had one too many glasses or bottles of beer and/or liquor. The truth serum had an immediate effect.

As a kid, I didn't fully understand how that related to me or how it significantly shaped her way of parenting. All I understood was there was a playground, I was a kid, and the two entities were meant to go together. They were a match made in heaven, like peanut butter and jelly, like socks and shoes, like DJs and turntables.

I was a very strategic young man, a chess master without the trophy. I'd do my best to get on her good side, so I used to clean up the living room or the entire apartment to win her over. Sometimes my tactics worked, but oftentimes it was just considered voluntary labor. Not one to be bored in the apartment all day, I kept myself occupied by creating board games (Monopoly) from scratch and fantasizing about what it would be like if I went on a trip to Disney World. My happy place.

Watching those Disney World advertisements as a kid took me to a faraway place where dinosaurs weren't extinct and elephants with big floppy ears flew. If only for a moment, I pictured myself in a magical world free from despair, and my imagination was allowed to run wild. Running through the park, I could see Mickey Mouse and Goofy by the teacup ride calling me to hop in. The smell of popcorn and cotton candy swam through the air while my favorite Disney tune serenaded my soul. Oh man, how I wished to be one of those kids on TV with a pair of Mickey Mouse ears on my head. I vowed that one day, I'd take a trip to Disney World. But for now, all I had was my imagination and a vow.

Playing games in the apartment was better than playing no games or having no fun at all. Rolling up two socks and shooting them into a clothing hamper like a basketball hoop was a popular game. We also watched some of our favorite cartoons, like *G.I. Joe*, *Thundercats*, and *He-Man*. My brother had a replica of Castle Grayskull and He-Man action figures. I loved to hide those too. Television shows like *The A-Team*, *Different Strokes*, and *The Cosby Show* were frequently broadcasted through our television set.

Karate or something like it was also another way my brother and I passed the time. I was Bruce Lee, and he was whatever no-named bad guy challenged my five fingers of death. One year, we got a Nintendo game system for Christmas, which upgraded our stay-at-home status. Although Joseph would probably tell you different, I was a master at playing Mike Tyson Punch Out, Super Mario Brothers, and Contra. We'd play video games for hours upon hours until we fell asleep or mom made us turn off the television, whichever came first. For those of you born in the '70s or '80s, remember when we had to blow into the Nintendo game cartridges to make them work? Fun stuff.

On the other hand, when mom went on a mission, she wasn't so anxious about us going outside to play. She seemed to be less worried about our well-being and more concerned with getting high. She would let my brother and me play outside well into the night without once calling our names out the window. This wasn't her usual behavior because on the rare days she did allow us outside, she would call us as soon as the light post came on so we wouldn't be out in the dark.

I could still hear her yelling our names out the window: "Jahan and Joseph time to come inside!"

"Ahh man," Joseph and I would complain, wishing for a moment that our names were something different.

I attempted to turn off the light post by kicking it in the right place to delay her call, which only worked on some nights. I guess the moon didn't align just right, and the odds were stacked up against me.

When I was in elementary school, I was frequently absent and not really engaged on the days I was present. I was encouraged to join every attendance-improvement program known to man. Also, I'd get the drill sergeant treatment from teachers, my friends, and administrators. And instead of telling a long story to each person who asked, I had one answer for everyone.

"Where have you been, Jahan?" they would ask. "We haven't seen you in forever and a day."

"I was sick," I'd reply. "I had to go to the hospital. I had a terrible case of uh, crackitis."

Although it was far from the truth, I wasn't too sure if they were genuinely concerned about my well-being or were trying to gauge the appropriate time to contact child protective services to remove me from my home. In the past there were two instances in which people from outside agencies visited us to check if we were living appropriately. They would check the cabinets and the refrigerator for food and ask us many specific questions related to how mom interacted with us. Most of the time we would put on a good show and lie to them, saying everything was fine. A part of me wanted to be honest with them, but I was too fearful of the consequences.

There were many friends I knew who were separated and relocated to live with other family members or strangers, and I couldn't let that happen. There were no guarantees that we would end up in a better family environment. I prayed that I didn't make a fatal mistake I'd regret. But at least we were together. My secret was safe with me. I locked it up and threw away the key. My teachers were unaware of all the drama I had to endure at home that negatively affected the way I performed in school. For instance, if I didn't get a chance to sleep well the night before a school day, then I'd more than likely have a "bad day" at school. There were times when sleep wasn't an option because mom had an altercation with the next-door neighbor at one in the morning or the dude snoring right next to her.

Stacey was the type of dude who could make Ike Turner blush. He picked up his hands more times to swing at a female than Pete Rose had hits. Stacey had a few missing teeth and some that were hanging on by a gum. He walked around like he was seven feet tall but only stood five foot eight. I had to Mills Lane a situation or two between him and mom. And from time to time, I had to tape up my hands, put on the gloves, and step into the ring. I was known for my bobbing and weaving but even more infamous for my two pieces and a biscuit: a jab, a right cross, and a punch to the gut combination.

Now, guess who was responsible for restoring order? You've guessed it! The police were responsible, although they rarely showed up or were on time. Public Enemy said it best when they rapped, "911 is a joke." Instead I played the role of a boy in blue minus the uniform, backup, and gun. I was in constant survival mode, and my behavior and grades in school began to take a dramatic turn for the worse. On a bad day, the last thing on my mind was solving mathematical problems or reading passages from a book.

"What's twenty divided by five?" my math teacher would kindly ask.

"Twenty divided by five equals your mother," I'd often angrily reply.

I reacted to any kind of situation angrily. All sound judgments were thrown out of the window. I was a ticking time bomb ready to explode at a moment's notice. My teachers couldn't engage me. I think it was because they were more concerned about the amount of days I was absent and how it affected the school's attendance percentage rather than the reasons why I wasn't present. No one was willing to delve deep into the root of my absenteeism. Children can feel when someone is genuinely concerned about them. You may be able to fool an adult, but a young person can see through a facade.

At home, I did my homework like I cleaned my room—fast and furious, with no attention to the details. Not only did I have to finish my homework, but I also had to help my brother and sister complete their homework. I understood the importance of an education, but I was too distracted by other things. Because of this, I passed most of my classes with the minimum grade required for promotion—a sixty-five.

How could I concentrate in school if I was constantly worried about my drug-addicted parent at home? I didn't know the answer to this question or who I could ask to reveal it, but my mind would often wander off to nightmarish places—the kinds of nightmares Freddy Krueger was based on. But this nightmare would take place in a Bronx project, not on Elm Street, as I opened the door to my apartment and discovered a gruesome scene.

My mom would be sprawled out on the living room floor covered in blood from a violent attack after a drug-related transaction gone wrong. Or would I find her face-down on the bed, foaming at the mouth due to an overdose on drugs? These were recurring thoughts on my mind. A penny for my thoughts would've made the poorest individual richer than the richest rich man.

I think I was slowly beginning to prepare my mind for the worst to protect my heart from the hurt of losing a loved one. It was sort of how at the age of twelve, I decided not to celebrate my birthday any longer because I didn't receive anything special on that day. The more I prepared myself for the worst-case scenario or didn't expect anything from anyone, the better I was able to deal with disappointment.

And there were enough disappointment to go around.

4

CALMS THE SAVAGE BEAST

Despite the passing of Uncle G almost three and a half years earlier, my days and nights still reeked of death and decay. The man with the red cape and big S on his chest never swooped in to save me. I guess his super hearing didn't detect my loud wails and faint sniffles. Those sons of guns in Metropolis are the lucky ones. Or maybe they aren't so fortunate. The good always attracts an element of bad like a superpowered magnet. But without the presence of bad, there can't be any display of good. So in essence, Superman thrives off of the bad because without it, how can he be super? Ironic, isn't it? Either way, I was in desperate need of a savior.

I scarcely made it out of elementary school, my dear Watson. I couldn't crack a case to save my life. I had no clues. My grades weren't the *greatest*. But at *least* I made it out on time, which was actually kind of late. I got held back in the second grade. I guess I couldn't quite get the math *right* so I got *left*. As a result, I was slated to attend my zone school, which was located right across the street from my elementary school. Most of my friends were going, so I was okay with attending. I figured it'd be a smooth transition. But unknown to me, I was predestined to be much more than a seventh grader.

The raging bulls sharpened their horns on the concrete to a fine point. They were preparing to charge as they forcefully pounded the ground with their hooves. The muscles in their front and back legs demonstrated their power. They had muscles stacked upon muscles like Pringles. This couldn't be happening. I was a matador, dressed in all red, waving a gigantic red cape that read, "Bully me." And the bulls were everywhere and on top of their game like the Chicago Bulls in the '90s.

I was like Marty McFly in the movie *Back to the Future,* forever finding creative ways to escape the clutches of a Biff. No hover boards were included. I had no super-juiced time-traveling cars at my disposal or mad scientists available to help get me out of a jam. Taking my revenge on all the Biffs of the world, I decided to stop running and began to fight back—with my mind, that is. I came up with different ways of defending myself other than with my fists.

I recall during the first month of school being approached by the son of a Sasquatch. This was the type of kid who would've taken the Gooch's lunch money and had his grandmother baking him cookies. This seventh grader had to be at least six feet tall and weighed two hundred pounds, with a size-twelve shoe. He resembled the boxer Clubber Lang (Mr. T) in one of the Rocky movies.

I could still see the smoke coming from his nostrils as he snarled and said, "Hey you, what shoe size you wear?" He asked it with the intent to see if it was worth his time and energy to take my brand-new pair of New Balance sneakers.

I nervously replied, "Eight and a half. My big cousin, Killer Mike, who's a certified black belt, bought them for me." That was the end of that conversation.

This is funny but not so funny.

You know how when you're about to fight someone much bigger than you and your friends are present, so even though you're scared to death, you put on a tough act? I mean scared to death like the bogeyman himself tapped you on the shoulder as you slept in your pajamas scared. Like the monster you swore hid in your closet and under your bed when you were five years old scared. We've all experienced it, whether we're white, black, or yellow. It's not a racial thing but more of a, "I don't want to get beat up, so I'm going to put on a show" thing. Some of my best work was the "don't hold me back" routine—the one where you pretend that the reason why you haven't thrown any punches yet is because someone is in your way even though no one is there.

"Yeah, you're lucky my friend is holding me back or else I would've gone crazy." Or we'd go around each other in circles shoulder to shoulder, saying, "Stop pushing me. No, you stop pushing me" until one of us would decide to swing or someone got in between to break it up. And I prayed for the break up.

I guarantee that most young people who talk tough about wanting to fight have a small voice inside of their heads saying, "Lord, if you stop this fight now, I promise I'll be good. I'll eat all my vegetables and clean my room every week." No one really wants to risk getting seriously injured.

I could've been nominated for an Academy Award for my performances. "In the category of best supporting actor in a street brawl, Jahan!" the announcer would say. I really wasn't afraid to fight, but I'd much rather avoid a messy confrontation. I only got into physical altercations at school when it was absolutely necessary. I didn't like getting suspended, staying at home for three days, and listening to mom rant and rave about my behavior in school.

It's important for me to mention that people who bully others oftentimes have been bullied themselves. They become aggressive toward others after experiencing years of intimidation. They begin to embrace the false sense of power behind making someone feel inferior, so they take on the bully role. Most would rather do the bullying than be the one being bullied. In fact, most people in general

Anthony Perseveres

try to exalt themselves to a higher stature by putting others down. It's a tactic that has been implemented since the beginning of time.

Here comes the commercial. If you're being bullied or know someone who's being bullied, notify a responsible adult immediately. It's not snitching. It's called helping a fellow peer in need. A quick lesson on snitching—snitches are people who tell on others in order to save themselves from some sort of consequence. The definition doesn't apply to individuals with good intent who inform the proper authorities that someone may harm themselves or someone else. Now back to our regularly scheduled programming.

In middle school, I dressed in the latest mid- to late-'80s fashions, wearing Levis jeans, polka dot shirts, farmer pants (with the Looney Toon characters painted on it), Jordan sneakers, and not to mention the hair. I had the best-looking flattop with a blond streak my middle school ever witnessed.

That's my story, and I'm sticking to it.

However, my taste in clothing and keeping up with the latest trends didn't match my appetite for learning. I wasn't engaged in school. I was more interested in being the next big rap star. I wrote volumes of black and white composition books of rhymes when I should've been copying down class notes and studying. If only I had known the odds of me getting a record deal were next to impossible. I had a better chance of getting struck by lightning, on a Tuesday, in

December, while riding a bike, singing "Old McDonald Has a Farm." This reminds me of how I initially got started with writing rhymes.

My fifth-grade math teacher, Ms. Tompkins, during the infamous jerry curl era, gave me an assignment to write a rap song. She was interested in teaching us how to learn math in a fun and engaging way through music. Excited about the challenge, I went home that night and couldn't wait to get started. I put my thoughts and ideas together and wrote them all down in my notebook. I went to school the next day, stood before the class, and recited my rap. A thunderous applause resounded. Ms. Tompkins looked over at me and winked. It was a sign that I successfully completed the task and met her approval.

The fire was lit.

I decided to write another rap song and another and another. And as time progressed, I got better at my craft. My delivery, flow, and lyrical content intensified. Throughout my rap years, I practiced most of my raps in front of my sister Jenny. She knew most of my lines better than I did.

I quickly gravitated toward rap music and the hip-hop culture because I easily identified with it. I walked, talked, and dressed like most of the rap artists of the '80s and '90s. Well, I didn't have the phat gold chains or the three-finger rings but … you get my drift. Rap music spoke directly to me. It was as if the rap artists had peeked into the window of my existence and wrote everything they saw and heard. Each song painted an accurate picture of my life growing up in the hood. The lyrics captured the rare moments of pleasure and the all-too-familiar years of pain. Through the music, I felt as if I wasn't the only one in the world dealing with the tribulations of life.

I also realized that the verses I wrote helped me to deal with the negative. I was able to get my emotions out on paper in a creative way. I was so sick and tired of crying about the ills that befell me. I needed to find a positive outlet to release my pain. Oftentimes, during periods of sorrow, when we're able to identify with someone or something, it helps us to cope with it. We all need to identify a positive outlet for releasing our negative energies.

Calms the savage beast.

I enjoyed watching videos on *Video Music Box*. Artists and groups like Wu-Tang Clan, Big Daddy Kane, Run-DMC, LL Cool Jay, A Tribe Called Quest, and Leaders of the New School were among my favorites. But singing along to an R&B song was my guilty pleasure. Nobody could tell me I wasn't R. Kelly when "Bump and Grind" blared through the speakers. But my vocals didn't match my enthusiasm for the art of soulful singing, so I stuck to writing rhymes.

At school, during lunchtime, I rapped over a beat that one of my friends drummed on the table. I also held a few sessions over a beatbox battling MCs in the boys' bathroom. The acoustics played to my advantage. It was like microphones were set up all throughout the restroom. You'd think that I didn't have a bathroom pass, but I did. The only problem was that I stayed much longer than the allotted ten minutes needed to conduct lavatory-related business. But every school MC, boy and girl, wanted to go head to head with me and my partner in rhyme, so we had to accommodate. We took on all challengers and handed out rap pink slips. We put an end to some rap careers before they even got started.

At home, true to what Biggie Smalls said in one of his rap songs, I played my favorite songs over and over until the tape popped. I even fixed them with scotch tape after they were damaged so I could continue listening to them. I had to salvage the few possessions I had because who knew when I would be able to buy another tape. And when buying a new album wasn't an option, recording a song off the radio station was the next best thing. I remember listening to the radio for hours waiting for a station to play a particular song so I could record it.

Wearing the traditional ready-to-bust-a-fly-rap gear that consisted of baggy jeans, construction-colored boots, and a hooded sweatshirt, I'd flip through the pages of my black composition notebook, desperately searching for a fresh, clean sheet to compose a verse. It called out to me, "I'm right here, Shag!" That was my rap name during my preteen years. At last, I found a blank page yearning for the ink in my pen to paint a lyrical portrait of emotion. Cracking my knuckles like Bruce Lee did before he executed a devastating roundhouse, I'd fall deep into a trancelike state and write bar after bar like a young man possessed. The words always seemed to pour out of me and onto a page like paint into a pan. A few bright coats overpowered the wall of darkness. The wall was one hundred feet high and painted jet black, so there was much work to do.

Like the day mom went on a mission and left us home alone for two days. We had no idea where she went and didn't know if she was safe or not. All I knew was that I had to assume my role as the eldest and take care of my siblings. It was during the weekday, so although we were supposed to attend school, we didn't go. I was afraid that someone at school was going to find out that mom was missing and take us away.

The first day was the most difficult because my brother and sister did not fully understand why mom wasn't present. I wanted to protect them so they wouldn't be worried, so I said that she was at a family member's house and would return home soon. At thirteen years old, I found myself having to cook, clean, and monitor my brother and sister carefully. I honestly find it challenging to cook a tasteful meal now, so you can imagine what it tasted like when I was thirteen years old, although I could boil a hot dog fairly well.

I was very creative, so I experimented with various kinds of recipes. The first night we were alone, I decided to make a dough bread jelly sandwich. Let me explain. I can't make this stuff up. We didn't have any bread in the apartment, so I made dough with flour and water and fried it in a frying pan with oil. I put some grape jelly on top of it and thought it was the best crispy jelly sandwich I ever tasted. It was the best steak and potatoes Smuckers never made.

The second day was more of the same. We had fried dough bread coming out of our ears. And the only thing pouring out of our hearts was worry. A few weeks prior, a drug dealer had come to our door and threatened to kill everyone inside the apartment. An unpaid debt prompted that warning. I was two seconds from calling the police and reporting her missing. Looking like she fought her way out of heck, she eventually came home that evening. Not a single word was uttered, so I let my pen do the talking and wrote a rhyme about how I felt. Thank Jehovah for rap.

As I advanced in age and my vocal chords began to produce deeper tones, I wanted some privacy, so I converted the living room into a third bedroom. But we had little to no furniture in the living room. Most of it was sold on the streets in exchange for money or drugs. I was good at making things work, so although we didn't have a fully functional stereo system, I managed to piece together some old stereo components in order to listen to music. I had to have my music. We also had two televisions, one for the sound and one for the picture. It was the type of TV you had to use a clothing hanger, stand on one foot, and sing "The Star-Spangled Banner" to receive good reception. There were no flat-screen high-definition TVs or over one hundred cable channels. No WHT or HBO for us. We were lucky to have a remote control.

Now that I think about it, I was the remote control. Mom would call me from the other side of the apartment to change the channel. Even Mr. Belvedere didn't have to change channels, and he got paid for his duties. But somehow, I was the channel changer, the take-your-shoes-off guy, the pour-me-a-glass-of-juice/water boy, and everything else in between.

I was so accustomed to responding to constant emergencies that I always slept with my boots and clothes on. Sleeping in full attire was a conditioned habit that lingered for many years. My wife would often remind me to remove my shoes before coming to bed. It was important for me in a house of chaos to not be caught off guard where I couldn't respond to a situation accordingly. I knew the drug dealers who knocked on the door during the day and night weren't stopping by to borrow a cup of sugar and have idle conversation. They were looking to conduct business and were only interested in collecting a debt or supplying a product.

I usually wore a black or dark-colored hooded sweatshirt, a pair of blue jeans, and construction boots. It wasn't only my rap costume but also my ready-to-beat-somebody-up-down- and-all-around outfit/ costume. And with it, I believed that I possessed all of Superman's powers without the weaknesses. Cracktonite had no effect on me. I was able to leap out of bed, put my boots on faster than a speeding bottle thrown from the eighth floor, and be stronger than two pit bulls playing tug of war with a tire.

Don't misunderstand me. I had a lot of patience, but it seemed to run paper thin at three in the morning. It was a rare occasion when I was allowed to sleep for eight hours straight. I was so prepared that I even made weapons to offset the fact that I was only five foot four and weighed 120 pounds wet, with boots on, and a 20-pound dumbbell in my book bag. Don't try this at home. But there was a cane that I kept by the couch that I named Betsy (I guess I was watching too much wrestling) and a spray can with a lighter attached to it like a mini flamethrower. Fortunately—for the person on the other side of the flamethrower, that is—I was never put into a position where I had to use it.

Rap music kept me close to her bosom and comforted me like a warm goose down quilt in the winter. She reminded me of a sit-down by the fireplace. I listened to the clicks and crackles of the firewood and watched as the flames danced around the logs. I was gratefully distracted. I almost forgot for a moment the rusty pitchfork that was slowly scraping across my gut. It sounded like the agonizing screech

Anthony Perseveres

from a long fingernail scratch on a blackboard. But she managed to soothe my soul from all the anguish life had to offer. Instead of lashing out at the first person I saw because of all the anger I harbored inside, I wrote a rap about it. Rap music managed to calm the savage beast within. It was my penicillin when I was ill.

And boy was I ill.

An ill lyricist, that is.

5

EXIT STAGE LEFT

Once again, there I was locked in the basement—an infinite maze of dizzying twist, turns, and abrupt dead ends. It was a dark and dreary place of despair. I was never afraid of the dark before tonight. I slept alone but felt safe and secure without a night-light. I threw away my false sense of security eons ago. The occasional bumps in the night didn't serve to alleviate my fears. They reinforced them. There's a scary monster in my closet. The clawing sound against the inside of my closet door was all the proof I needed. *He's probably eight feet tall, with razor-sharp fangs and nine-inch claws—the perfect type of talons to tear my brown flesh to tiny bite-size pieces. It feels like the four walls are slowly closing in. I'm trapped without a means of escape. I'm doomed.*

With a black garbage bag full of clothes, a backpack stuffed with unfinished rap songs, and a certain uncertainty, I traveled on foot the twenty minutes it took for me to get to my titi Maria's house in the Bronx. She owned a two-family house, and I was going to take up residence in the semifinished basement. I counted the number of sidewalk seams I passed on my way there.

I'll only be one thousand or so sidewalk squares away from them, I thought. *Maybe I should just turn back. Maybe I'll just cope with the drama a little while longer.*

Praying that I didn't sink like a ton of bricks and drown, I decided to jump ship. I needed a place of solace to rest my weary soul. So at the age of fourteen, with my mother's blessing and my tia Maria's permission, I gathered the few possessions I had and moved in with her and my older cousin, Rico. Although I was petrified to leave my younger siblings behind to deal with all the monster-type issues that lurked around corners, hid in their closets, and dwelled under their beds, I believed that in order for me to improve my family's situation, I had to move out. As the eldest, I understood that it was vital for me to position myself in a manner that would allow me to properly care for my siblings. And I couldn't position myself well in what I felt was a little- or no-opportunity situation.

I was driven by the idea that one's level of happiness is determined only by the degree of one's effort. And I needed to put a lot more effort into my pursuit of all things good. Happiness wasn't simply bestowed upon individuals who desired it. It was to be sought after and maintained accordingly. Easier said than done.

I found some relief in the fact that my brother and sister were only a hop, skip, and a brief walk away from my aunt's house. Still, I felt especially guilty for leaving my sister, Jenny, because she was only seven years old. She needed her big brother like a flower needs the sun's rays and water to grow. I felt like my departure significantly dimmed her light. It also cut off ample water supply to her roots. My guilt was as thick as the cheese sandwiches I used to make.

If we allow it, guilt will hold us back from freeing ourselves from strenuous situations. We often feel obligated to stay or participate in particular activities for fear of guilt or shame.

But was it really my responsibility to take care of my younger siblings to the degree that I missed out on my own childhood? Possibly not.

Was I supposed to be my brother and my sister's keeper to the point that I kept track of their every move while severely neglecting to monitor my own maneuvers? Maybe so. The selfish part of me just wanted to be a kid. I didn't ask for any of this. *None of this is my fault,* I thought. But I had a great deal of faults to correct. I passed most of my middle school classes through a series of miraculous acts and gifts bestowed upon me by the giver of grace. I understood that it was my responsibility to step up my academic game. Practice makes an individual that much more prepared. No more riding the bench for me. I wanted to be counted among the starting five.

The Mount Everest–like climb in front of me was intimidating. I know many who've attempted and failed miserably to scale her peaks. I was far from an intermediate climber, but I was determined to plant my flag at the summit and obtain a high school diploma.

In today's society, I understand that getting a high school diploma may seem like a natural occurrence for most, but my generation was full of high school dropouts. But I realized the importance of staying in school and performing well academically. I knew that those who are smart usually go far in life. At least that's what I heard on TV, from my teachers, and from some of my family members. And I really wanted to go far in life.

At Titi Maria's house, the rules were simple: go to school, get good grades, and stay out of trouble. Titi Maria, a Department of Education–licensed teacher, emphasized how important it was for me to get a good-quality education. But I really didn't follow the rules accordingly. Although I was there to do something better with my life, I quickly took another stance, especially since my cousin Rico wasn't going to school. I sure wasn't willing to go to school and miss out on the day's festivities, like chilling in an empty two-family house with a group of girls three or more years older than me, playing a friendly game of spin the bottle. How could I resist, right?

When I moved in, I was entering my freshman year of high school. A week or so before the move, my uncle Larry stopped by to visit and blessed me with $300 to go school shopping. Uncle Larry was just cool like that. He would pop up from time to time and share the wealth. He gave me my first bike and set of weights and let me borrow his car on occasion for a couple of days at a time. I was the only eighteen-year-old in my neighborhood driving a gold Maxima like I owned the road.

The Bronx high school I attended was a large school of seven floors and thousands of students. I came from a small middle school of just four floors, so I wasn't used to navigating such an immense area. As you can imagine, during the first few weeks of school, I found myself lost and late to every single class—not to mention all my classes were jam-packed with students, many of whom were not interested in what the teacher had to say. Maybe it was because most of the teachers moved at a fast pace and only seemed to speak to students in the first few rows. Or maybe it was because it seemed as if some of my peers were only present in school/class to socialize.

Either way, I was caught in the middle. I found the material very difficult to grasp. My math class was much like my science class— absolutely painful to watch, hear, and attempt to understand. I sat in the back of the class with the rest of the eventual dropouts staring into oblivion on some days and pretending to jot down detailed notes on others.

And so it began …

I decided I'd rather miss a day or three of school than have to deal

Anthony Perseveres

with all of that nonsense. The situation was way too uncomfortable for me.

During my first year of high school, I played on the junior varsity football team. But I was only in school long enough to attend a few practices and play in two games. I was absent so many days from school that I couldn't grasp the lessons taught by my teachers. I didn't even know any of my teachers' names after the first year. Thus, I fell even further behind in school because I missed so much instruction. I was so embarrassed and ashamed to sit in class because I felt lost. And because of this, I failed every single class on my schedule and was kicked off the football team. If I had been able to receive a grade for lunch, I would've failed that too. I even failed gym. How do you fail gym? All I had to do was come prepared with the proper attire and participate. I couldn't pass a course to save my life.

Thus, my academic status went from promotion in doubt to promotion not going to happen. I had to repeat the ninth grade. My titi Maria was very disappointed in my academic performance or lack thereof. She told me that I had to shape up or ship out of the basement, so I vowed to do much better the next academic school year. Only time would tell.

My cousin—Rico Suave, that is—and I were very close and still are to this day. There weren't many boys our age in our family outside of my brother and a few male cousins we really didn't communicate with. We relied on each other and connected like brothers. We did everything together—cut school, spoke to girls, got into fights. We were not the type of kids to join gangs. We were more into being around girls and looking fresh instead of joining a gang.

Rico is the true definition of a pretty boy, with all the luxuries that come along with that title. He had the mutant-like ability to talk to girls with absolute confidence and vigor. I refer to it as mutant-like because it's unusual, downright abnormal, for a human being to possess such powers at eighteen years old. He was like Professor Xavier's little nephew. He masterfully wielded the power of mind control to the tenth power.

But maybe it was his curly black hair that constantly swayed in the wind that made it so easy for him to secure the digits of a female walking down the street, up the block, or around the corner. Or maybe it was his light-skinned complexion, which seemed to glimmer in the sunlight, thereby mesmerizing members of the opposite sex to hand over the digits. Whatever it was, he'd approach a female as if he already knew she was going to give him her name and phone number.

"Excuse me, miss," he would say in a Billie Dee Williams–type voice. "I just had to walk over here and meet you. You're absolutely gorgeous."

Then, utilizing the Jedi mind trick, he'd wave his hand in front of her face and say, "You want to give me your name and number." And

Anthony Perseveres

with no hesitation, girls would reach into their purses and scribble their names and numbers on anything they could find. Cousin Rico was a young man way ahead of his time.

I thought my direct experiences with dealing with someone on drugs had ended when I moved in with Titi Maria. But I was naive to believe that the nightmare was over. A family member lived with us for a short time and was also addicted to crack cocaine. He sold not only his stuff but also other people's belongings in exchange for money. He would sneak into Rico's bedroom as he slept, unplug the VCR from the wall, grab the beeper lying on the table, and sell it to the highest bidder on the street.

Rico and I would track him down at night, as well as the goods he sold. We would say to ourselves, "What would a crackhead do in this situation?" We were like two Puerto Rican Columbos canvassing the neighborhood, looking for clues, and identifying suspects. I felt like I couldn't escape it. Everywhere I went, the ghosts of crack cocaine followed me.

And they were very scary ghosts.

Most of them had drawn-in faces and little to no teeth and wore tattered clothing. They smelled like train smoke and alcohol and developed some form of a nervous twitch. And with the stamina of an Olympic gold medalist, they just kept going and going Energizer bunny–style. It was like watching *Night of the Living Dead* as they walked up and down the neighborhood like zombies. It was as if they came straight out of the Michael Jackson "Thriller" video without the fancy dance moves and red leather jackets.

They would sell anything they could get their hands on, even themselves (or someone else), to achieve a higher plane of what they considered to be ecstasy. Nothing was off limits. I once saw a crackhead on the block attempting to sell her baby's formula. The craving was too great a force to be denied. But I couldn't just blame the addicts. It wasn't all their fault. I also wasn't too fond of drug dealers.

I viewed them as the scourge of the earth regardless of the major reason why some attempt to rationalize the sale of illegal drugs—to support their families. How could someone sell something so harmful to another person that is destined to bring about disaster for an entire family? Disaster on both sides of the coin: drug dealer and abuser. Heads or tails? Both parties will lose. A drug deal gone wrong or a feud over territory can easily spell tragedy for a nonparticipating, innocent family member. I guess the idea of making a quick buck is worth the risk.

On a positive note, all of this kept me away from experimenting with any kind of drug because I was too afraid of being hooked on it. I felt like it was a disease I could easily contract if I got too close. There were too many examples around me of the negative effects of drugs and alcohol. I didn't want to become another victim trapped in its spell.

Although I promised my aunt to perform better academically, my second year in high school was more of the same. I continued to play hooky and make up 101 excuses for why I couldn't attend or stay in school.

Either I got up too late, had no clean clothes, couldn't find my bus pass, had a stomachache, headache, foot cramp, nosebleed, or leg itch, the work was too difficult, or the weather was too hot or too cold.

So instead, my cousin Rico and I would stand on the corner in close proximity of the high school and talk to all the girls who passed by, trying to get their phone numbers. The Force was strong with cousin Rico and me. Although I spent most school days on the corner, the days when I managed to make it inside of school were interesting.

I'd sit in the back of the classroom (cracking jokes, throwing paper, drumming beats on the table) doing everything I wasn't supposed to be doing. I was the type of student teachers and the administration loved to hate. I know they cringed on the days I showed up for class and thanked their lucky stars on the days I didn't show up. I was a permanent fixture in the cafeteria during fourth, fifth, and occasionally sixth period—not because I was hungry and needed to eat but because I was uninterested in math and science class and needed to waste time. And in a school among thousands of students, it was fairly easy to get lost and fall through the cracks. And if I didn't feel like staying in school at all (which was usually the case), I'd sign in for homeroom and then leave out the back door. Nobody stopped me or asked me where I was going.

Once again, I bombed every class and was slated to repeat the ninth grade for a second time. I was extremely embarrassed to have to repeat the same grade a second time. Also, feeling self-conscious, I felt like I was too old to sit in a class full of fourteen-year-old freshman. I had a mustache and a goatee, which made me stand out among the baby faces. *Everyone's going to laugh and have crazy jokes on me,* I thought. *They may mistake me for one of the teachers. No mas.* I waved the white flag and dropped out of high school at sixteen years old.

I exited stage left and self-reflected.

I was standing tall in front of the mirror, a chiseled image of infinite style and swagger. I was proud of the person staring back at me. But I often wondered if I resembled my sperm donor. If the way my jawline was cut was an exact replica. If the thickness and pitch-black color of my eyebrows were the direct result of his genes or if the signature bop in my walk and the sound of my voice were directly inherited from him. The angry young man in me hated the notion that there was an atom of a chance that I had anything in common with my biological sperm donor. I'd rather gouge my eye out with a rusty fork dipped in acid rather than share a single cell with him.

But sometimes I found myself daydreaming, wondering how tall he was or if his complexion was anywhere near my shade of brown. I wanted to feel and say that I was better off without him, but the truth was, I wished he was man enough to be a man—man enough to be a father. Why didn't he want me as his son? Did he not like the way I looked? Was my hair a little too coarse or my eyes a little too bright? Was it something I did or said? Did I ask for too much milk or drop my bottle way too many times? I just couldn't figure it out.

Sometimes we try to rationalize why things happen or do not happen to us. And we oftentimes blame ourselves for why people harm us. I needed to stop making excuses for him and be okay with the fact that he wasn't present in my life. But it was difficult to let it go.

Maybe one day, through the power of divine intervention, I thought, *I'll bump into him on the street and he'll recognize me as his son. And maybe, just maybe he'll have a perfectly good explanation for not being around for the past sixteen years of my life.* I may have been willing to accept that a plane went down at sea and he had been living on a deserted island eating coconuts. Or he had a tragic accident that resulted in a coma. Anything short of that was unacceptable.

I clearly didn't have any kind of relationship with my biological sperm donor. The fondest memory I had of him was going with my mother to family court when I was five years old to prove paternity. And although it was confirmed without a shadow of a doubt that he was my father, for some reason or another, he decided to abandon his daddy duties.

He exited stage left.

But as Jehovah would have it, one evening on their way home from work, my abuela and titi Maria bumped into a former colleague who had contact information on how to reach my father. They shared the information with me and stressed the importance of me reaching out so I could find some sort of closure. My immediate reaction was a negative one. I didn't think he could teach me anything I didn't already know. I taught myself how to tie a tie, shave, and buy a suit. Plus, I didn't think that our meeting would result in a positive encounter because I had so much anger and hostility toward him for being a coward. I was forced to grow up faster than what was generally expected of a kid. I felt like I was sixteen going on twenty-one years old with all the problems I faced.

After a week or so, I ultimately decided to reach out and arrange a time and place to sit and talk. Besides, I did have a slew of unanswered questions to pose. I viewed it as an opportunity to get all that weighed heavily on my mind and heart out in the open.

So, I met my father for the first time at sixteen years old. To make a long story short, I moved in with him and my two younger siblings, only to return home to the projects a few months later because of a heated verbal altercation he and I had. Interestingly, another sixteen years passed before I saw him again. Maybe I'll see him for a third time when I turn forty-eight years old.

I believe that many individuals we come in contact with throughout our lives are only meant to be with us for a season. Whether we care to accept it or not, they're only present to teach us something specific about ourselves, like how a good or bad relationship can help us learn to appreciate ourselves or others more. I think we must take opportunities to reflect on the significance of their presence and how it applies to our own lives.

We must learn from each and every interaction and add the experience to our quest to become better individuals.

6

HOW DIAMONDS ARE MADE

I could sum up my entire childhood in three words: the Dark Ages. Never would I wish what I had to endure on my worst enemy. From as far back as I could remember, I was fighting for my right to grow up as a child free from despair. I fought vigorously. I was thrown into the pit of fire with a pair of gasoline-soiled pants on. Diamonds are made through extreme pressure and intense heat, so I guess I'm no exception.

As a high school dropout at the age of sixteen with no secondary education, I had to settle for any job (at minimum wage) I could secure. I thought if I wasn't going to be in school, I should at least have a job. I was a foot messenger in Manhattan for a day. I think you can deduce with a great deal of accuracy why that didn't pan out. After a full day's work, my dogs were barking louder than four pit bulls in a Chinese restaurant. I know you're probably thinking, *Four pit bulls in a Chinese restaurant? Why would a dog bark in a Chinese restaurant?* Well, I guess you have to live where I lived to understand the reasoning behind that concept (dogs usually bark when cats are around). Nonetheless, I was worn out because I walked for hours and for miles carrying packages up and down hundreds of flights of stairs. Also, the hustle and bustle of a crowded New York City street took a toll on me. There were people loading and unloading trucks and yellow taxi cabs dashing in and out of lanes.

Plus being the directionally challenged person that I am, I got lost half the time. Yeah, I know that being a longtime resident of NYC, I should know my way around, but you'd be surprised how many people can't navigate through their own neighborhoods without a GPS. Growing up, only once in a blue moon did I venture outside of the Bronx. My first trip to a Manhattan museum was when I was twenty one years old because I had to complete an assignment for an Earth science course.

Many young people of color who live in impoverished neighborhoods seldom leave the confines of their block. They're reluctant to explore areas outside of their zip code for fear that an inevitable danger is lurking around the corner (which is often the case) or because of plain ol' ignorance (which is more often the case). Fear of the unknown is one of the main reasons why we don't take initiative to learn new things. Our unconscious minds want to keep us in a box. I was afraid of failure, so I refused to give it my all in school. We're often so afraid of being labeled nerds, so we earn Cs and Ds to remain cool while the "nerds" get all the good grades and excel in life.

Sitting idle and being too afraid to take steps toward learning something new is far more dangerous than what may be waiting around the bend. The best advice I was given a long time ago is to "do it scared." This means, despite how fearful we may be to attempt something that is new and challenging, if we believe the task is worth our time and energy, then we must participate and "do it scared." Anything worth anything gives us a little anxiety because it means that much to us, which is a normal response.

Working in the freezer section of a supermarket as a meat packer taught me a lot about physical as well as mental toughness. I developed a greater appreciation for individuals who worked in extreme weather conditions. I understood how a frozen chicken felt (if a frozen chicken could feel anything at all). My work attire consisted of a long white lab coat that was designed to protect me from the arctic winds but only got in my way. I had my daily routine down pat. I'd grab a box of drumsticks packed in ice and place eight of them in a clear plastic bag. Then I twisted the bag, weighed it, and stuck a price label inside of it. And the more I did it, the more I realized that something had to change for the better.

I really didn't want to spend the next twenty or more years working in jobs that didn't pay enough money for me to do the things

I wanted to do. Also, I didn't want to devote my precious time to working hard in jobs that I really didn't have a passion for. If working hard meant an improved lifestyle, then I was all for it. But hard work seemed to only get me blistered fingers and an aching back.

I didn't know what my next step would be and what direction I was headed in, and my titi Kimberly told me about a government-funded program that would allow me to live in a college-style dormitory, receive free room and board, obtain a GED, and learn a trade.

The youngest of six children, Titi Kimberly was the best aunt a nephew could ask for. She didn't have the greatest sister-to-sister relationship with my mother, but that didn't affect how she related to me. Without question or judgment, she would welcome me and my black garbage bag full of clothes whenever mom decided to kick me out of the apartment. She lived a few floors above us, so I just rode the elevator up to the twelfth floor. A definite shoulder to lean on, she listened to me talk for hours about my current situation and what I wanted to do when I grew up. And with that, she would always refer things for me to take advantage of.

A vocational training center sounded like the perfect opportunity for me to shine like the sun on the hottest day of the summer. I understood some time ago that for me to increase my worth and get a good-paying job, I needed to acquire some work-related skills as well as an education.

I recall sitting on the edge of my bed in the basement and once again thinking to myself about the potential harm my siblings would face in my absence, especially since for the past two years, when I visited my mom's apartment, I noticed that things were getting increasingly worse. I needed to do something radical. I needed to partake in something that was considered to be life-changing for the better. Hence, I made the conscious decision to attend the center. But not before I spoke with my cousin Rico, who agreed to check in on my siblings from time to time while I was away. I felt good about that. He was someone I could trust. He was a man of his word.

So, the next day, mi abuela took me down to the placement office in the Bronx and signed me up to attend. Two weeks later, I was scheduled to leave for the center. The night before my departure, I packed one army bag full of clothes and personal items, had a long conversation with my siblings about where I was going and why, and prayed to Jehovah that I was making the right decision.

The next morning, mi abuela met me downtown at the pickup site in Manhattan and wished me good luck as I boarded the bus for the eight-hour trip to Buffalo, New York. But little did I know, I would be taking an hour-long airplane ride to Buffalo, New York. The bus I boarded was headed to the airport. Did I mention that it was the first time I flew in an airplane? I was more scared than being in a lion cage with a steak suit on dipped in barbecue sauce. But I had to

Anthony Perseveres

face my fear. I did not know what to expect at the center, but my goal was to learn a trade and obtain my **GED**.

The center was a very interesting experience to say the least. Upon my arrival, I was anxious but at the same time ready to take on a new challenge. The campus was located in a remote area surrounded by woodlands and natural habitats, something I wasn't exactly used to living in the projects, but I embraced it nonetheless.

I lived in an all-male dormitory in a suite-style living quarters with seven other young men of Latino and African descent. It was a tight space, but I made the best of it. I had a closet, a bed, an army fatigue outfit or two, and steel-toed boots—not to mention, three square meals a day and a monthly allowance to purchase clothing. I had all the necessities needed to survive. I was cool with my suitemates and most of the corps members on campus.

It was a very strict environment. There was zero tolerance for disruptive behavior and negative ways of being. If there was any indication that you were involved or possibly would be involved in something menacing on campus, then you would receive a one-way ticket back home. In fact, with no time to waste, you were given no time to pack. All of your belongings were sent to your home in the mail. During my one-year tenure, many young people were handed their walking papers and were quickly replaced by someone else looking for a new lease on life.

Like the time a male student got into a heated discussion with another male student and decided to impersonate A-Rod at the plate by introducing his head to a pool stick. Not exactly how the New York Yankees bat practice, but he found it effective. At least in his mind, it was an immediate solution to his problem. Thus, he received his walking papers faster than the ink dried on the paper it was printed on.

Or the time a bunch of male students beat up another male student for "talking too much." He got the living snot kicked out of him. Thus, ten or more students received their walking papers. I kept myself as far away from trouble as humanly possible. I had too much to prove to myself and all those who doubted my ability to become successful.

The center wasn't for everyone, but I made it my business to adjust and fit in. Some corps members were ready for a life change and committed themselves to staying positive, while others picked up from where they left off in their neighborhoods. The bully continued to bully, and the troublemaker stood on the straight and narrow path toward finding trouble.

I know you heard of the saying that you can accomplish whatever you put your mind to. Well, that's half of the process. You also need to put your heart into it. The heart is where the true change for the better solidifies. It begins in your mind but needs to transfer and deeply root into your heart. You must believe that you can improve your current situation.

Say it out loud! "I am somebody who will accomplish a great number of things!"

Allow your mind and heart to embrace the idea that you're worth the change for the better, that you're worth "getting the good" out of life. Because oftentimes, when we are constantly faced with the bad stuff, we don't know how to embrace the good when it comes along.

I guarantee that once it reaches and embeds in your heart, there's nothing or no one that could tell you different. You begin to say and do things that you never thought were possible. I had to constantly remind myself that I was there for a bigger purpose and that I deserved a second chance. I couldn't allow the guilt and shame I felt from not doing well in the past keep me from my ultimate goal. Too many of us let the rut of our current circumstance bind us and dictate our future. People make mistakes. We all make mistakes. The thing that counts is how you learn and make amends for those mistakes.

The staff at the center took their jobs very seriously. They woke us up every morning approximately at six o'clock and gave us firm instructions. And they didn't do it by gently tapping us on the shoulder or giving us a little nudge but instead with a beaming flashlight on our faces and a deafening roar that nearly blew out our eardrums.

"Everybody wake up!" screamed the dorm director. "It's time to make the doughnuts!"

They were referring to the fact that we all had to get up, clean the room and assigned dorm area, take a shower, get dressed, eat breakfast, and arrive at either school or trade by eight in the morning. I wasn't used to that kind of discipline and responsibility. In the beginning, I took it personally, as if no one could tell me what to do and how to do it. But I constantly reflected on my motivation for being there in the first place. I was firmly grounded in my responsibility to my siblings to be a positive role model.

How diamonds are made.

The structure was one week of school and one week of vocational training. I chose to study carpentry. I hated to acknowledge it, but my father did have a positive impact on me after all. In his home, he had a carpenter's workshop full of tools and a bunch of woodworking projects that sparked my interest. His vocational skills led him to secure many jobs as an electrician, cabinet maker, carpenter framer, painter, and plumber. He was a true jack-of-all-trades and a master at many of them.

Without me even realizing it, he instilled in me how important it was to have a good work ethic. And it wasn't what he said that stuck with me but what he did. Actions definitely spoke louder than words. I unintentionally took mental notes about how hard he worked from sunrise to sunset and never once groaned about it. I actually learned something from the time he took me to work with him so I could earn my own money and appreciate the value of a dollar. My role was to do most of the demolition cleanup, but he capitalized on opportunities during breaks to share trade secrets.

He introduced me to the wide world of carpentry, and I was captivated by the feeling creating and building things with my hands evoked. I was delighted by the sense of accomplishment I felt through the process of developing an idea in my mind and physically making it come to life. I discovered something new and more importantly something that I was good at. And I didn't even know that I was good at it. But imagine if I didn't even open my mind to explore the possibilities and at least try to learn something new. There are hidden talents within all of us that are just waiting to be discovered.

While at the center, I participated on a track team that literally took me places. It was the spring of 1994, and for our first official track meet, we headed out to SUNY Buffalo to compete against other vocational training centers within New York State. I was scheduled to race in the four hundred–meter and hundred-meter dash respectively. Even though I ran my little heart out, I didn't come in first, second, or even third place. My first track meet was my last track meet. I came to the conclusion that running was an activity best suited for exercising and people who knew how to do it well.

The campus was amazing to say the least. There were various academic buildings, cafeterias, and dormitories spread out as far as the eye could see. It was a city within a city. The streets and sidewalks were spic and span, and the environment felt safe and peaceful. In fact, the campus was so clean that I saw students sitting on the grass reading books. No one sat on the grass where I lived to do anything, not to mention to read a book. Even the air was different. Maybe because there were so many trees.

I watched in amazement as students of all nationalities socialized with one another. Caucasians, Asians, Latinos, and African Americans were actually walking, talking, and eating together. They all seemed to be united toward achieving a common goal—a college degree. Back home my neighbors were only shades of brown and yellow, so I wasn't accustomed to seeing such diversity or people of different ethnic groups coexisting.

Most of the Caucasian people I came in contact with were by coincidence of the mass transit system. In fact, the extent of my interactions with individuals of a much lighter persuasion was sharing a train car on the way to our destinations. Interestingly, I learned a trick that many people of color are familiar with when a train is too crowded and you want to get a seat: stand next to a Caucasian person sitting because his or her train stop is coming up soon. If you're coming from downtown Manhattan to the Bronx, then any train stop along the way will guarantee you a seat. Well, let me rephrase that. Any train stop along Manhattan will assure you a seat. As a kid, I always wondered why that trick worked until one day I actually got off at Fifty-Ninth Street and it all became clear.

The neighborhood was lush with green vegetation, and the streets and sidewalks were clean. There wasn't any broken glass on the ground or cigarette butts in the grass. Liquor stores weren't on every corner. People were walking their dogs. It was a pleasant atmosphere—an atmosphere that I felt like I deserved to live in and an atmosphere where I felt like my siblings, family members, and friends deserved to reside.

While on campus, to make sure I wasn't just imagining what I saw, I asked a student in the dorm if everything was real because at seventeen years old, it was my first real-life introduction to college. I felt like I was in the Lost City of Gold. My eyes were opened wide, like Adam and Eve in the garden of Eden when they first realized their nakedness. Never did I imagine that such a place existed where young people of color were able to live and learn in a safe environment without having to look over their shoulders. But I couldn't fathom that such a place was accessible to me. Surely a place like this cost much more money than my family could ever afford.

My first introduction to college (if you can call it that) prior to the trip to Buffalo University was watching the television show *A*

Different World. The show was a spin-off of *The Cosby Show* and focused primarily on African American students at a university and all the interesting antics that went along with college dorm living.

I remember watching that show and saying to myself, "I wish I could go to college. I want to be in a fraternity and live in a dormitory too."

However, it was a dream that I decided at the time would remain just that—a dream. I had no idea that college was something available to me and that I could actually attend an institution of higher education. No one in my family (other than Titi Maria) received a college degree, so what made me think I could?

I had more questions than I had answers. Despite my inability to answer these questions, the foundation was laid. I was exposed to a fraction of what an institution of higher education had to offer. And I wanted it bad. My soul was set on fire. I was tired of failing, so I decided to do my best at the center.

And I did.

7

BACK TO SQUARE ONE

When I returned home from the center, I was almost eighteen years old. After one year, I obtained my GED, driver's license, and carpentry certificate and had a few thousand dollars in my pocket. I had a new lease on life because I finally felt like I had accomplished something great. Before this, I had failed at almost everything I attempted to do, so it was my first indication that I innately possessed what it took to do something well. Sometimes all we need is a flicker of hope to be set on fire. Once you've realized your true potential, your confidence level will rise to astronomical levels. Nothing or no one will be able to stop your trudge ahead.

The eight-hour bus ride home from Buffalo, New York, to the projects gave me an opportunity to seriously reflect on what my next moves would be to improve my life as well as the lives of those close to me. Looking out the window, I envisioned securing a full-time job as a carpenter framer and making enough money to move out of my mom's apartment and take my siblings along with me.

There was no way in heck I was going to return home to the same old story because coming home from the center during the holidays made me aware that mom was still on a mission playing the same type of character (Dr. Jekyll and Mr. Hyde) she had been playing for the past eight years. And it seemed like a never-ending story.

It was known to some as the day we ate like lions. The Thanksgiving dinner I will never forget is etched into my memory for not-so-good reasons. You know how typical thanksgiving holidays include an abundance of food, drinks, music, and family, right? Well, my house was the exception. Mom was a wonderful cook, but one day as the formula was consumed and the pinky twitched, she went on another mission. Somehow her next assignment was given to her in the middle of preparing Thanksgiving dinner.

As a result, she abandoned her cooking responsibilities and didn't have an opportunity to cook anything other than meat. No macaroni and cheese, rice, or potato salad. We had turkey, chicken, and pork shoulder sandwiches and soup for about two weeks. At least we had food, unlike so many other people in the world, but we were concerned about not having sweet potato pie and rice and beans.

Because of this, and countless other situations, I knew I had to act quickly and put a plan into action as soon as I touched down on Bronx soil. The week I arrived, I began searching in the yellow pages for construction companies for hire. It was a technique I had learned from watching my father look for jobs. I called twenty or more companies until I stumbled upon one that needed to hire a carpenter framer.

The job was located in Long Island City. I was hired to lay floor bricks in a fancy-smancy house and build a bunch of cubicles and partitions in an office building. I only stayed with the company for a couple of months. The owner took complete advantage of the fact that I was young and inexperienced and only had a secondary education. He paid me $7.50 an hour, which was way below the standard of $15.00 or more an hour for a carpenter framer. I quickly realized that I didn't have the work experience and level of education required to demand what I deserved financially.

Although I was making some decent money (as long as I didn't have to pay rent, that is), I really wasn't on a career path to increase my earning potential. I repeat—I said that as long as I didn't have to pay rent and other bills, the money I earned was decent. You see, many young people who live with their parents believe that if they drop out of high school and get a job, everything will be fine and dandy. I assumed that as long as I got a job that it didn't matter if I had a high school diploma. After all, a job is a job, right? It seemed cool for a moment because I didn't have many financial responsibilities. But nothing I was doing was going to significantly change my living situation for the better. Nothing I was doing was going to "rescue" me out of poverty and catapult me into the lifestyles of the rich and famous.

Please understand—there's a Grand Canyon–like difference between having a job and having a career. Jobs are usually meant to last for a season or a short period of time, while careers typically span a person's lifetime. It's like the difference between owning a home (career) and renting an apartment (job). As a renter, you pay X amount of dollars to a landlord each month. The money you pay doesn't increase the value of your rental. In other words, your money isn't really working for you or adding to your worth. On the other hand, homeowners pay a mortgage that, in light of the recent housing market disaster, is supposed to increase the value of your ownership. Pursuing a career is an investment into your future with all the benefits attached at you and your family's disposal. I had zero benefits—no healthcare or 401(k) plan, dental or vision insurance.

But how was I going to pursue a career? Earning a GED was a great step in the right direction, but I still didn't have the education necessary to pursue a viable career. I wanted more. I came to the conclusion that a college degree determined how much money one would make and the type of benefits that are available.

Over the next two years or so, I worked in a number of jobs as a means to maintain some sort of income. I was no stranger to hard work, so I managed to juggle a job or three at a time.

I worked for a touring bus company cleaning and painting the inside and outside of what seemed like endless amounts of double-decker buses.

And ...

I worked at a nursing home mopping and sweeping floors and cleaning the bathrooms from top to bottom.

And ...

I worked for UPS sorting and stacking packages in truck, after truck, after truck.

And ...

I worked as a painter and or carpenter completing small fixer-upper-type projects here and there.

And ...

I worked as a camp counselor at a nonprofit organization working with kids who were five to eight years old.

I had no clue as to what career I wanted to pursue or how to do it, but I was certain that I needed to advance my education. I was at a dead end.

Back to square one.

By the time I turned twenty years old, I received some horrible news. Joseph was arrested and charged with committing a serious crime. He got involved with some bad people and was sentenced to serve thirty years in prison. At the time, we didn't really have a close relationship with each other. Nevertheless, he was my little brother, and I loved him. I was devastated by the news because there was nothing I could do to save my brother from this fate. My initial feeling was that I had failed him and that I didn't do my job as an older brother to protect him. How could I let this happen? Was there something I could've said or done to prevent this? I wished for a long time that I had been present the day he committed the crime as a voice of reason.

The thing that made his sentencing so hurtful was that he had a promising career as a rap artist. Although I introduced him to rhyming, he stuck with the craft and surpassed my ability. The way he put together songs and delivered each verse was magnificent—far better than most of the rappers who were on the radio at the time. He was a rap genius way ahead of his time. I know he's going to read this and gloat. I'm never going to hear the end of it. You don't know how many times I thought about deleting it. But it's Jehovah's honest truth.

This is a teachable moment. It's important for you to not allow your emotions to get control of your actions. Uncontrollable anger is a dangerous fuel that leads many to crash and burn. Don't be afraid to walk away from a situation. Most of the "tough" individuals I knew who attempted to solve problems with their fists are no longer with us. They are either six feet deep or six feet behind concrete. Physical altercations never solve anything. Instead they escalate a problem to more serious matters. The best course of action in a heated situation is to remain cool and think about the consequences. I know it sounds easier said than done, but I assure you that if you don't think about it before you act, you'll have plenty of time to think about it locked away. Making split-second decisions could affect you for a lifetime.

At this point in my life, everything seemed to not go according to plan. I went away for a year and returned home with some accolades that were supposed to put me in a great position to win. But I felt like I was losing. There was a loud knock at the door.

"Who is it?" I shouted.

A deep voice on the other side of the door responded, "My name is Keith, and I have some important information to share with you about Jehovah's Kingdom. Do you have a few minutes to discuss it?"

I peeped through the peephole and saw a gentleman dressed well with a Bible in his right hand. Although I was very reluctant, something told me to open the door and hear what he had to say.

After sitting and talking with Keith, who was a Jehovah's Witness, I was convinced that I had found salvation. I began to read the good book every night before I went to bed. I was on a personal quest for knowledge and understanding. Within these scriptures, there must be an explanation for my plight and a way for me to overcome it, I thought.

This couldn't be the way I was meant to live and die. Was I destined to fail? I hadn't seen much success and hadn't known many people who were successful. I was compelled to find the answers, so I searched the Bible for guidance. I poured my heart out to Jehovah in prayer, hoping for a sign of better things to come.

My findings gave me a renewed outlook on life and all the grand possibilities it had to offer. Hope was restored. Deep down in the very pit of my soul, I believed that Jehovah would find a way out for me. I just needed to rely on Him and allow the path to salvation to be shown—sort of like Dorothy on the yellow brick road but I was more like the Tin Man. A little oil (the word of God) here and there when I got rusty (tired and worn down) was just what the doctor ordered to keep me going. Keeping the faith was more than just a belief; it was an action. In other words, I needed to prove with action the extent of my faith. And just when things could've gotten worse, they got better.

As twenty-one years of age approached, like every other young adult growing up in New York City, I enjoyed attending social events here and there. One night my cousin Rico and a few friends and I attended a social event that led me to a special someone. Well, I actually went to a nightclub on the east side of Manhattan. I tried to make it sound decent (social event), but it was nightclub—a

Anthony Perseveres

typical fog-smoked, strobe-lighted, music-louder-than-it-needs-to-be nightclub. It's the kind of place you shouldn't think about visiting until you're old enough to vote plus five more years.

As I entered the club and began to canvass the dance floor to see which lady I was going to invite to dance, the DJ began playing one of my favorite R&B songs. And at that moment, my eyes caught a glimpse of heaven. I saw her standing only a few feet away from me. She was a shade or two from being light-skinned. Her complexion was more like the color of caramel. Her hair was silky and smooth, and she wore bangs that fell just above her eyebrows. Her eyes were electric—I mean Ben Franklin flying a kite, wearing a tin hat electric.

I felt like I was in the presence of a modern-day Mona Lisa. And with the smoothness of a Latin Casanova and the delicate touch of a doctor holding a newborn baby, I reached out and grabbed her by the hand. Then I pulled her close to me, and without saying a single word, she knew just what I wanted. Her beautiful smile was all the confirmation I needed to proceed. So, I spun her around, dipped her once, and caught a whiff of her sweet-smelling perfume. A hint of White Diamonds filled the air. We locked eyes, and she was immediately smitten by my charm and finesse.

I asked her to tell me her name, and she said, "My name is Ms. Caramel, and I'm only here on earth for a day. The Lord sent me to you, so no longer do you have to pray."

And from that day forward, we lived happily ever after. Well, that's how it played out in my head, but that's not what actually happened.

Only in the movies.

I must say that my dance techniques have improved over time through trial and error—a whole lot of trial and error. I recollect the days of the "robot" when I attempted to be cool at a neighbor's birthday party but only managed to look constipated.

"Jahan, are you okay?" a concerned partygoer in the back of the room asked.

"Yes, I'm okay; can't you see that I'm dancing?" I replied.

"It looks more like you need to use the bathroom than dancing," he jokingly responded.

"Nobody asked you, so mind your own business," I scoffed. "This is the new improved robot, R2D2."

But those days were far behind me. I'm not saying that I went from Rerun to Fred Astaire, but I gave her my best version of the two-step with a twist—a little Latin flavor of Sazón and sofrito. However, after a song and a half, she deserted me and made her way to the second floor. I felt like she dropped me like a bad habit—like she was drinking too much caffeine and needed to quit cold turkey. I expected to dance with her for at least two to three songs. I wanted to maybe buy her a drink or three and get her phone number. But no luck. I stood there with my face on the ground trying to figure out what went wrong. I felt like the prince after Cinderella left him at the ball. But at least she left him a little glass slipper.

I sped walked to the restroom and checked my breath with the blow in your hand and inhale breath test and concluded that everything was in order. The spearmint Tic Tacs in my front pocket had taken care of that a while ago. Confused and frustrated, I eventually took it as a loss and quickly two-stepped my way back onto the dance floor.

Two hours later, looking as fine as I want to be, I was approached by a young lady who wanted to know my name and number. She walked up behind me and tapped me on the shoulder. As I turned around, I realized that it was Ms. Caramel. With a Cheshire cat smile on my face and my heart beating like the drums on a J Dilla track, I welcomed her solicitation. I took out a piece of paper from my front pocket, wrote my name, and number on it, and the courting began two days later with a phone call—a very long phone call.

I guess I was a bit smitten by her. I'd travel two hours on the train from the next-to-last stop in the Bronx to the last stop in Brooklyn. Two hours each way! It was a total of four hours' travel time just to see this girl. Actually, it took more than four hours. I had to take a ten-minute bus ride to the Bronx train station on 233rd Street, get on the train for a two-hour train ride, and then take another ten-minute bus ride from the Brooklyn train stop to her parents' house and do it all over again on the journey back home. A staggering four hours and forty minutes of travel time. But when you're young and in love, you'll do just about anything your heart dictates. You'll swim the Nile River without a life jacket, climb the Himalayas with only an ice pick, or walk across the Sahara Desert barefooted to get to the one you love or like a lot.

This reminds me of a time when my innocence was evident in the way I related to girls. When I was a preteen, all I really wanted to do was say that I had a girlfriend. Although I wasn't quite sure what having a girlfriend actually meant, I knew that I had to have one because all the cool guys or the ones I thought were cool talked about all the fun they had with their girlfriends. I remember the first time a girl asked me, "Do you want to go out?" There were some really bold girls in my elementary school. I immediately said no, thinking my mom would never let me "go out" with a girl. I couldn't go outside in front of my building, let alone take a girl out somewhere. I had it all twisted up and mangled like a ten-car pileup. A few weeks later, a close friend of mine explained to me what going out actually meant. And as a result, I started going out or dating.

Prior to meeting this amazing woman, I dated a number of girls, some who were significant but most not worth mentioning. I'm not going to pretend like I had a whole bunch of girls on my team, but I did have a few franchise players. I was a bit shy, so I didn't have any unique pickup lines or creative ways of approaching girls. But the one thing that was consistent and I was good at was being myself, which is difficult for most people to do—be themselves. The worst thing you could do in any social situation is to attempt to be someone or something you're not. Pretending is a sure way to keep your friend or significant other count at its lowest. Always stay true to who you are. No one can be a better *you* than *you*.

She eventually became my wife and bore two sons. I mean, that's what smart men do, right? They marry the woman who makes them feel good about themselves. Many of us spend a lot of time worrying about finding someone special to share our lives with. First of all, it's important to remember that the ones who are "special" usually come along when you're not looking. A good way to determine if you've found that special someone is to give him or her the "Jahan test." I thought of the name as I wrote this.

The Jahan test is simple: If you're down to your last dollar and your significant other is willing to take it, find someone else. If you're in a tense situation that may result in a physical or verbal altercation with someone and your significant other encourages you to handle it violently, find someone else. If most of your conversations with your significant other are negative and never seem to focus on anything positive, find someone else. If your pursuit to be that much more positive is often discouraged or not even supported by your significant other, find someone else. Never settle for less than you deserve.

You deserve a great deal.

People will treat you the way you allow them to treat you. Be sure to set high expectations for how you should be treated.

8

THE GREAT EQUALIZER

The late '70s gave way to a boy of Latino descent who was born into a tumultuous world full of haves and have-nots. And from the onset, it seemed to the boy that many were destined to remain on a particular track not by choice but due to life circumstances.

He grew up in a rough neighborhood where showing how tough you were was just as important as how many points you could score in a basketball game. His priorities were far from being in order. They were out of synch, out of whack, and extremely unproductive.

Despair was like a dark cloud that forever lingered in his bedroom. And he couldn't seem to escape the black cloud of toxicity that invaded his every sense of being. It flooded his lungs and made him sick to the point where he began to not see the true value in reading a book or solving a math equation. He was too engulfed by all the distractions, distractions, distractions life had to offer.

Before I knew what a college education could really do for me, I was in the dark about the doors it could open. I didn't equate one's level of success to one's level of education. But after completing the vocational training at the center and working a couple of years in various occupations, I realized the importance of obtaining a college degree. I understood how it would help elevate me out of my difficult living situation.

Education is the great equalizer!

I wanted more than just a job; I wanted a career. With that realization, my vigorous search for a good college began. Plus, since my girlfriend, Ms. Caramel, was currently attending a four-year CUNY college, I was positively peer pressured to also attend an institution of higher education. But my GED could only take me but so far. I never made it past the ninth grade, never sat for a regents' exam or an SAT exam, and never took any advanced placement courses.

I was at a disadvantage.

Because of this, I didn't initially meet the minimum qualifications to be admitted into a four-year college, so I had to begin my college education at a two-year school.

In my search, a close friend who was also conducting his own college search told me about a two-year community college. More than anything, I was intrigued with the school's location. The campus was located in White Plains, New York, which was a good distance away from all of the distractions of the city. But it also meant that I had to endure a grueling commute. I had to take a bus to a train to another bus. I thought it was worth it, so I called the school and made an appointment to meet with an admissions and financial aid counselor. And to my surprise, I met the minimum requirements to be admitted into the school.

I was ecstatic!

I was amazed!

I was anxious!

I was humbled!

I enrolled for the first time in college at twenty-one years old.

If you recall, a few chapters ago, I mentioned that one of my weakest subjects was math. The placement test I took confirmed that I needed to take a remedial math course and a college-level English course.

I was so nervous on the first day of school.

My hands were sweaty and a bit shaky as I walked into my first-period English class. I located a seat somewhere in the back of the classroom, sat down, and took it all in with a deep breath.

"I am a college student."

I wasn't sure what that really meant, a college student, mainly because I hadn't been much of a student for the past ten years. Should I attempt to write down everything the professor said? Should I do my best to answer every question posed? Should I make it a priority to participate in all discussions? Should I wear my prescription frames to appear that much more intelligent?

I looked around the classroom and immediately noticed a few things. I was one of only two students of color. I kind of expected that. Most students had five subject notebooks. I didn't get the memo. And most students already had the required textbooks for the course. I was still waiting for my financial aid check to arrive, so all I had was a composition notebook in my book bag and a number-two pencil pressed firmly behind my ear.

I'm already behind the eight ball, I thought.

But I also thought if I made it through the vocational center, I could make it through this. I constantly reflected on my past accomplishments as a means to motivate myself toward achieving other great things. When self-doubt appears, we must remind ourselves of times when we were successful. It serves to dim our self-defeating thoughts and shed some light on the ones that uplift us instead.

As a first-generation college student, I was in need of a great deal of guidance. I needed someone I could speak with about all the ins and outs of the college experience in terms of the proper ways to study, time manage, and organize. All the other things related to the "college experience" I figured I'd learn on my own.

Fortunately for me, all the poems and rhymes I wrote kept my mind and pen sharp. Although I lacked the necessary skills to write a proper sentence from an academic perspective, my English professor took interest in my enthusiasm for learning and ability to write a good story. He took me under his wing and set me up with an English tutor a few times a week. Every paper I wrote, Dr. Costa made it mandatory for me to see someone from the writing center to review it word by word, sentence by sentence, paragraph by paragraph.

Dr. Costa made me realize that if I really wanted to be successful in college, I had to work at it. I had to put forth the right amount of time and effort to reap a great reward. I needed to fully integrate myself into the college experience. I spent countless hours on campus working with various tutors, completing assignments in the computer lab/library, taking advantage of work study opportunities, talking with my professors about my progress and what I could do to perform better, participating in school-related activities with my peers, and getting acquainted with the various offices and individuals around campus that were available to help support students. After my first semester, I managed to achieve a 3.7 GPA (A-) and was placed on the dean's list.

I was excited!

I was surprised!

I was thrilled!

I was humbled!

It made me realize that I had what it took to succeed in an institution of higher education. My confidence level in my ability to perform well academically continued to build brick by brick. By the end of the academic school year, I maintained a 3.5 GPA (B+).

Around this time, I ran into a distant cousin, Doris, who sparked my interest in attending college away from home. She worked at a nearby SUNY processing center that was just a few blocks away from where I lived in the projects. She insisted that I make an appointment to sit and talk with her. In our meeting the following week, she spoke of all the wondrous things an away college had to offer. She cleverly catered to the youth in me and mentioned all the clubs, parties, and fraternities I could participate in. But she also highlighted the importance of me having time away from the things I was already familiar with in order to explore new and exciting things. Our conversation made me think back to my visit at Buffalo University and how much I enjoyed being on campus. I was truly intrigued.

In disbelief about my chances of being accepted to a competitive away college, not to mention being able to afford it, I shrugged it off.

Yet Doris encouraged me to take a placement test at the center to assess my academic skills in preparation for a competitive university, and I reluctantly agreed. When the test results came back nothing less than stellar, she highly suggested that I look into applying to a competitive university. So I did.

The anxiety in applying to a prestigious university took me back to the first time I performed on stage.

Butterflies filled my stomach and slowly crept up my chest as I stepped out onto the stage. It was the biggest stage I ever saw. I was nothing but a mere guppy in the middle of the Atlantic. The lights were so bright that I could feel the intense heat beaming off the bulbs onto my face. My palms were sweaty, and my legs were shaking like rattles. The place was jam-packed. There must've been at least five thousand people present waiting to see me perform. I'd prepared for this moment for months. Practicing in the mirror with a brush for a microphone kept my rhyming skills sharp—sharper than a Ginsu. At least I hoped.

It was probably not the best time to think about flowing water, but my nerves were getting the best of me. I pictured a slow drip from a leaky faucet and the sound of raindrops hitting a drain spout. I didn't need to use the bathroom before the curtain opened, but now I felt like a two-year-old about to do the pee-pee dance. "I've got to hold it," I said to myself. I went over in my head all the techniques used to decrease stage fright. Don't look directly into their eyes. Picture everyone naked. Find a focal point in the back of the theater and concentrate on your performance. Not sure what would happen—whether I would get booed off the stage or receive a standing ovation—I approached the microphone and tapped it to make sure it was on and spoke.

I waited for what seemed like forever for an admission decision letter from the university. Some of my friends told me that college acceptance letters came in big envelopes while others told me that they came in small ones. I wasn't sure what to think. I instructed everyone in my family to find me the moment the mailman arrived so I could be the first one to open my mail and read it. Every day I anticipated the arrival of the mail and the letter that would determine the next forty years of my life. A college acceptance was the difference between life and death for me. I was dying to get in so I could get out and live. When the letter from the university finally arrived, I couldn't read it.

"Just open it and tell me what it says," I told my mom as I paced back and forth, rubbing my hands together and trying to calm my nerves.

"Are you sure you want me to read it?" she asked.

"Yes, please just read it out loud for me," I pleaded. "Wait a minute! Let me do it. Matter of fact, just lay it down on the table for a moment."

Anthony Perseveres

I read the first paragraph at least five times before it officially registered in my brain. I was accepted to the university. I cried, ran around the apartment, and dropped and rolled like I was on fire.

"Yes, I am out of here!" I yelled at the top of my lungs.

I couldn't wait to get on that Greyhound bus and ride my way to freedom. I couldn't believe that I was accepted to one of the most prestigious universities in the country. The acceptance letter in my hand was my golden ticket—Willy Wonka epic. The university actually wanted me as a student to sit in their classes and take their courses.

My initial anxieties proved to be a waste of pondering. I thought away colleges were only meant for rich kids. But it seemed as if I would be able to afford the tuition cost after all. The government grants and student loans I had applied for made it all possible. Also, because of my mom's financial situation and my grade point average, I was eligible to enroll as an EOP (Equal Opportunity Program) transfer student. The program gives students of color who fall into a particular income bracket financial assistance as well as academic support.

Sometimes we don't ask questions because we're afraid to ask them but also because we don't know what questions to ask in the first place. Until I began to conduct my own research, I did not know that the government gave out monetary grants (money that doesn't have to be paid back) for college. It's vital to your life progression that you seek out information. Not everyone is going to tell you everything you need to know about something. Do your own research.

Living in a college dormitory three and a half hours away from the Bronx for the next two or more years was a big deal for me. Despite my worries, every sense of my being told me to go for it. For the first time in my life, my heart was aligned with what my mind was thinking. This was something much bigger than me. I was also motivated to go away because my girlfriend, Ms. Caramel, was already attending her first year at a university in upstate New York. She transferred from a city college of New York City and set her sights on pursuing a college degree from a state university.

As an EOP transfer student, I was required to attend a four-day summer program on campus that gave me a head start on what the university had to offer. I took the Greyhound bus from the Port Authority and arrived at the university a whole two months before the official start of the fall '99 semester. Through the EOP program, I was able to meet over one hundred students and staff, get acquainted with the campus, find out who my roommate would be, and get an idea for the courses I could take in the fall. It was a great experience.

The night before I was slated to attend for the fall semester was bittersweet. Here I was the first one in my family to attend a university, and I was miserable. I procrastinated and waited until the last minute to pack. That night, I just couldn't sleep because it reminded me of the day I left for the vocational training center and all the mixed emotions I had about leaving. After all, my mom was still on a mission.

Every important decision you make in life will play tug-of-war with your conscience. The only sensible thing for me to do was to get down on my knees and pray to Jehovah to guide my footsteps and keep my sisters safe.

So I prayed, "Lord, I surrender all to You. You have been there for me since the beginning. I ask that You continue to walk with me and keep a watchful eye over my sisters. In the name of Jesus Christ, amen." That simple prayer comforted me because I believed every word would come to pass.

That morning, my titi Kimberly arrived in a go-cart to pick me up and take me to the university. We stuffed her tiny car with as much college-ready material as possible and hit the road. I put my license to use and drove half the way. Three and a half hours later, we pulled up to the dormitory I was assigned to reside in.

Over the next two and a half years, I participated in various activities on campus and was in turn introduced to a number of individuals whom I call amigos to this day. I followed the same formula (full integration equals connection to greater success) I used to be successful during my time at the community college. I made it a priority to familiarize myself with as many socially related activities as humanly possible. Notably, I was an executive board member in a club that catered to the idea that young people from New York City who were considered to be "at risk" could benefit from a mentor and a two- to three-day stay at a university.

As a full-time college student, I had to work part-time to keep my pockets properly laced with dinero. The financial aid I received from the government didn't cover all my financial needs. Some students were fortunate enough to not have to worry about where their next dollar was coming from. Not that I was losing any hair over it, but I was somewhat concerned.

I was a credit collector for almost a year. The annoying voice on the other side of the phone that harasses people for a payment—that was me. Not one of my proudest work-related moments, but it served its purpose. I also found a job working with kids at an after-school recreational center. I found the job the good old-fashioned way—by searching through the yellow pages. I attended summer school two years in a row and was employed for one of those summers as a peer counselor for incoming EOP freshmen. My experience as an executive board member, peer counselor, and recreational specialist really grounded me in what I wanted to do as a lifelong career. I realized that I had a passion for serving at-risk youth. In fact, I spent my last semester as a university student interning at a juvenile detention center in New York City.

I could write story upon story detailing the great and not-so-great times spent at the university. Instead, I'd rather speak to some of the important pieces I learned on my journey toward graduation.

I realized that the people who manage to graduate from college are ones who have a fierce mental toughness. Not to say that intelligence isn't an important factor, but it's your capacity to socially, emotionally, and psychologically deal with obstacles that determines your overall success in and outside of the classroom. Finding creative ways to deal with the "pressures" of college life is essential. It solidifies who will walk across the stage on graduation day with ecstatic smiles on their faces or who will peep through the window with displeasure in their hearts.

They have a good sense of how to balance work and play. Too much "play" and one could end up on academic probation. On the other hand, too much work can leave one tense and extremely stressed out, which is not good for the soul. You must find the middle ground between work and play and make it a priority to cater to them both.

They know how to access information even when it's not readily available to them. We live in a digital age where all information of the known world is at our fingertips. You must utilize the "seek and you shall find" method of doing things.

They're not afraid to ask questions or ask for help when needed. Every person on this lovely planet of ours, at some point in their lives, has needed some assistance from someone. You must practice humility often. You'll be surprised what a little humbleness can get you.

They don't lose hope when the A grades slip and turn into Cs or Ds. Instead they shake it off and bounce back by finding academic support in the form of a tutor or study group. We all have our bad days or off semesters. Don't exhaust your time and energy dwelling on mishaps to the point where you're unable to move forward. You must adjust to your situation and adapt to it accordingly.

By the time I was a junior in college, I declared my major. I wanted to pursue a degree as a double major in sociology and Africana studies. I wasn't really sure what I wanted to do with the degree specifically, but … I was interested in the concept of society as it relates to human development and behavior.

To say that I worked my tail off in college is a gross understatement. I was a pure beast. King Kong had nothing on me. I said it years before Mr. Denzel won an Oscar for declaring it in a movie. I'd been training relentlessly for years. I beat my chest, roared, and swatted at all the airplanes that hovered above.

But I refused to go out like Kong.

9

FAR FROM FINISHED

The wind changed direction. I could smell the skunk-like stench of a Sith near. Each breath he took was long and deep. He must've been tracking me for miles. I quickly drew my light saber and stood firm in a Jedi fighting stance. Through the thickness of the mist that covered the area, I could see the enemy only a few yards away with his sights aimed directly at my vitals. But I was fully prepared because the force was with me. No Sith lord from the dark side could stop me from completing my mission. No Jedi mind trick needed. I was surgical with a light saber. I was a young Padawan with the skills and heart of a master Jedi.

"You've come all this way to try and stop me!" I yelled. "I'll be more than happy to disappoint you."

The enemy approached me from the rear and blasted a single shot that singed the left side of my head. My quick reflexes allowed me to dodge the hot beam of light just in the nick of time. I stared directly into his crimson red eyes as I raised my light saber over my head, preparing to inflict a lethal counterattack. I rained down on him like a category ten hurricane with all the strength that it embodies. And as he laid there on the ground mortally wounded, I rejoiced in the fact that another enemy was on his way to meet my Maker. But my joy was short lived as I turned around to see an imaginable sight. A vast number of enemy troops had gathered. The drama was far from finished.

You could probably guess that *Star Wars* is among my favorite movies. The story line provides an excellent way to illustrate the battle between good and evil—a fight I had to wrestle with the majority of my life. Evil lurked around every corner. It seemed like the good in my life came at a cost. I always had to go through the bad before I could bask in the glow of goodness. I eat Dark Vader–type problems for breakfast and spit out solutions. Despite all the bumps in the road, I was determined to obtain my degree by any means necessary.

Because I am a resilient, black Latino!

In fact, I'm a mixture of three distinct peoples. The African, Spaniard, and Taino Indian blood that flows through my veins unmistakably defines me as a Puerto Rican. However, growing up as a black Latino who spoke and understood a little Spanish, I struggled with finding my identity. Actually, people found it difficult to categorize me. I knew who I was, but people wanted to put me in a box. It wasn't enough that I said I'm Puerto Rican because I didn't sound or look like one according to what a standard Puerto Rican should look like. I lacked the curly hair and light skin. I was brown-skinned with a little less-than-coarse hair.

In the eyes of many Latinos, if you're Latino and can't speak and/or comprehend Spanish then you've violated the one thing that is sacred. It's an abomination that a Puerto Rican can't speak Spanish fluently. No excuses, but I'm a third-generation Latino in the United States. My grandmother was born here in the early 1930s.

I was tired of people sounding like a broken record: "You're Puerto Rican and you don't speak Spanish?" I thought if I lived in a Latin country, I'd be able to speak Spanish fluently.

"It's a long story," I'd reply. "You've been living in New York City for more than twenty-five years and you still can't speak English?" I'm just saying.

But I recognized how important it was for me to speak Spanish, so I made it my priority to learn. On my quest to becoming a better Latino, I took three Spanish classes in college that took me from only listening for my name in conversations to understanding how to conjugate. After three semesters, I was able to understand it more than I could speak it. It was a far cry from having a meaningful conversation with someone who spoke Spanish fluently, but it was a step in the right direction.

My experience dictates that most people living in America firmly believe that all Puerto Ricans are light skinned. Thus, if you don't have light skin and claim to be Latino, then the assumption is that you're Dominican. Here's a quick lesson in ethnicity. Puerto Ricans come in many colors, from my cousins who are Wonder Bread white to some who live on parts of Puerto Rico that are crayon-in-the-box black. This is why people of color are called just that—people of color. We represent many shades of colors.

The thing that defines me as Puerto Rican isn't the way I act or speak or how I dress but that I'm knowledgeable about my history and culture. Plus the fact that my mother and father are both Puerto Rican had a little something to do with it. Why do I have to prove my nationality? I am what I claim to be. If I walked around with a Puerto Rican flag tied to my head playing the congas, would that make me more Puerto Rican? I think not. Now that I got that off my chest, I shall proceed.

Life as we know it is made up of obstacles that take on many shapes and forms. When you manage to overcome one, another one takes its place. It's just like the old-school video game Tetris where, if there's a space that can be filled with a block, one shall occupy it. But what makes obstacles necessary to the human condition is all in how you handle them. You can view them as a means to become stronger or allow them to stop you in your tracks. As human beings, we have the unique ability to assess our roadblocks and decide to either jump over, go around, or crawl underneath them. We should view each obstacle we overcome as a triumph that adds to our resiliency.

Early on, I was cruelly introduced to what my life was going to be like for the next X amount of years. I was still in kindergarten when an army was sent in the form of a virus to murder me. The meningitis riddled throughout my system was relentless. But the medicine the doctors gave me found a cure. Jehovah knew that I was destined to do something incredible. So a new path was laid.

I was far from finished.

Graduating from college was one the most challenging tasks for me to accomplish. I was constantly faced with feeling overwhelmed and wanting to give up. And it wasn't because the courses were so difficult. I must confess that the occasional twenty-page paper did present a level of difficulty, a degree of stress, and patches of unwanted gray hair. But it was mainly all the strenuous stuff happening outside of my courses that weighed heavy on my mind, body, and spirit.

This was probably one of the most difficult sections for me to write in the whole book (sigh). So many intense emotions are attached to the next few paragraphs that it took me a few weeks just to get it all down. Then it took me another few weeks to fully process what I wrote. The constant pause in recalling painful memories and wiping away pints of tears made it difficult for me to stay on track. I actually tried to avoid writing it. At first, I tried to rush through it and just jot down what I wanted to say, but it didn't feel like I gave it the proper justice.

Much like the first, second, and third time I decided to leave my childhood home in the pursuit of happiness, my sister Jenny was once again left alone to fend for herself. Fire and brimstone accurately describe her unfortunate circumstance. She occupied my thoughts frequently. While at the university, I used every opportunity in my free time to call home and check on her and my other two sisters.

Jenny would always tell me that things were okay. But I could tell by the stressed, high, and low tones in her voice that she wasn't telling me the whole truth. And the most difficult thing about it was that I knew she was lying, but I couldn't do anything about it. I knew mom was standing right next to her with that crack-a-glass stare. Plus, things were never great, so how come all of a sudden everything was going well once I left? There was a small cry for help behind her enthusiasm to speak to me. The greater she said things were at home, the more serious I knew it really was.

To this day, no matter how many times I ask Jenny for forgiveness— and she looks at me like I'm insane for asking—I can't seem to find it in myself to forgive me. I know I did the right thing by leaving the

Anthony Perseveres

house to better myself to help my siblings but … There's a part of me that wishes there was another way to have handled it—that I could've stayed at home, remained sane through all the madness, protected my siblings, and made mom "well." But I wasn't a magician. All the Houdinis and David Blaines of the world weren't enough to make it all better.

Deep down in my heart, I felt like it was my responsibility to make things right—that if I didn't do something about it, then all would be lost. But what I didn't understand was that the problems that existed in my family were much bigger than me. They were much bigger than any child or young adult is capable of understanding and far beyond a child's ability to solve. The belief that I could fix everything was an unrealistic way of thinking. It was unfair of me to hold myself solely accountable for fixing the plight of my family.

Despite all of this, the sky was the limit in my book. If I worked hard enough, I thought good things would happen. Studying at the vocational training center and the community college taught me that. I needed a college degree like air to breathe, so I pushed myself to stay focused on the mission.

Although walking across the stage at the university as a graduate was one of the single-greatest moments in my life, it almost didn't happen.

The weekend I was slated to participate in the commencement ceremony at the university, a tragic event occurred. I borrowed my titi Kimberly's car, loaded it up with my loved ones (Ms. Caramel, Titi Maria, and mi abuela), and began the three-and-a-half-hour ride to the university. But as I merged onto a highway near Fordham Road in the Bronx, I was rear-ended by a guy driving a Cadillac.

Boom!

I slammed on the brakes, but the force from the collision was too great. The car skidded forward and crashed into the back of a car that was directly in front of us. I could still hear the terrifying screams as all the women in my life who meant something special to me feared for their lives. I could still see their arms flapping wildly as their bodies were tossed around in the car like rag dolls. Their heads bobbed around uncontrollably like the Derek Jeter bobblehead that once sat on the dashboard. I could still smell the burned rubber from the skidded tires.

It was a horrible scene that lasted only a few seconds but felt like a millennium. As the car came to a screeching halt, my first instinct was to look to the right and behind me to see if anyone was hurt. I prepared myself for the worst-case scenario. My grandmother and titi Maria were tough cookies, but they were in their late sixties.

Thank Jehovah we weren't "too cool for that safe belt." Mr. Kanye West said it best. There were no visible signs of injury, but just

Anthony Perseveres

as a precaution, everyone went to a nearby hospital for a complete checkup. The trunk of the car wasn't the only thing wrecked. I was an emotional mess as I watched everyone individually placed on a stretcher and hauled off to the hospital.

The accident confirmed it. I decided to not go to the university and attend my graduation. I was too distraught and couldn't focus on things that evoked happiness. However, the most important women in my life wouldn't allow me to throw in the towel. My abuela, from her gurney, looked up at me and expressed the need for me to attend to represent not only myself but the entire family. The next morning, Ms. Caramel, my titi Maria, my abuela, and I hopped on the Greyhound bus to the university. My mother and Titi Kimberly met us the following morning just in time for graduation.

My face felt numb. My bones ached, and my muscles were sore from all the climbing. Although there wasn't much oxygen for my lungs to absorb thousands of feet above sea level, I found a few precious breaths in tiny pockets of air that ensured my survival. After three and a half years, my perilous journey to the top of Mount Everest was complete. I finalized it by firmly planting of my flag at the summit. Red, white, and blue were clearly visible through the white snow. The view from the top was awe inspiring. I could literally stretch out my hand and touch a cloud. I was physically the closest man on earth to Jehovah.

I'd lost a lot of friends along the way, but I stood steadfast and weathered the elements. They handed me the key to open the door. It was not just any door. It was *the door*—the one to which only a chosen few were privileged to have exclusive access. I'd heard stories of a door like this only as a child. My teachers had spoken of such things, but never did I imagine this. The door had to be at least twenty feet tall—constructed by a master carpenter, no doubt. It was made of agar wood, and the door handle was comprised of pure gold. The only thing that was more interesting was my finding out what was behind it. Surely a door of this size and splendor was hiding something magnificent. At the top of it were words in small print that read, "Welcome to the land of opportunity." The moment I'd been waiting for had finally arrived. I put the key in the hole, turned the knob, and walked through. I made it. The trek toward obtaining my undergraduate degree was a tumultuous one. But it was only the beginning.

As I pen the final words of this book, I'm somewhat satisfied with my life's progression thus far. I say "somewhat satisfied" because I'm off to accomplish the next goal. I constantly set goals for me to reach and exceed. Three college degrees later, I'm still hungry for knowledge. I'm still thirsty for learning. I see a PhD in urban education on the horizon. I still make it a priority to reinvent myself

Anthony Perseveres

as a means to provide adequate services for our young people to succeed. There's still much work to be done.

I'm far from finished.

My story continues to be written. Pages are forever added. The chapter titles are bold, and the words are aggressive. I write story upon story to deliver a powerful message. I hope you've received it. It's never too late to do the right thing. It's never too late to get your life back on track. It's never too late to change an unfortunate circumstance into a blessing.

Be incredible, and do the unexpected!

ABOUT THE AUTHOR

Anthony Perseveres is the father of two amazing sons and the husband of a loving wife. He grew up in a poor neighborhood in the Bronx, New York. He earned a bachelor's degree in sociology and Africana studies, a master's degree in guidance and counseling, and a master's degree in school building leadership. He dedicates his life to helping at-risk youth and spreads the following message: "One's unfortunate situation doesn't dictate one's future."

Made in the USA
Lexington, KY
13 April 2018